THIS BOOK BELONGS TO:

_____

_____

TABLE OF CONTENTS

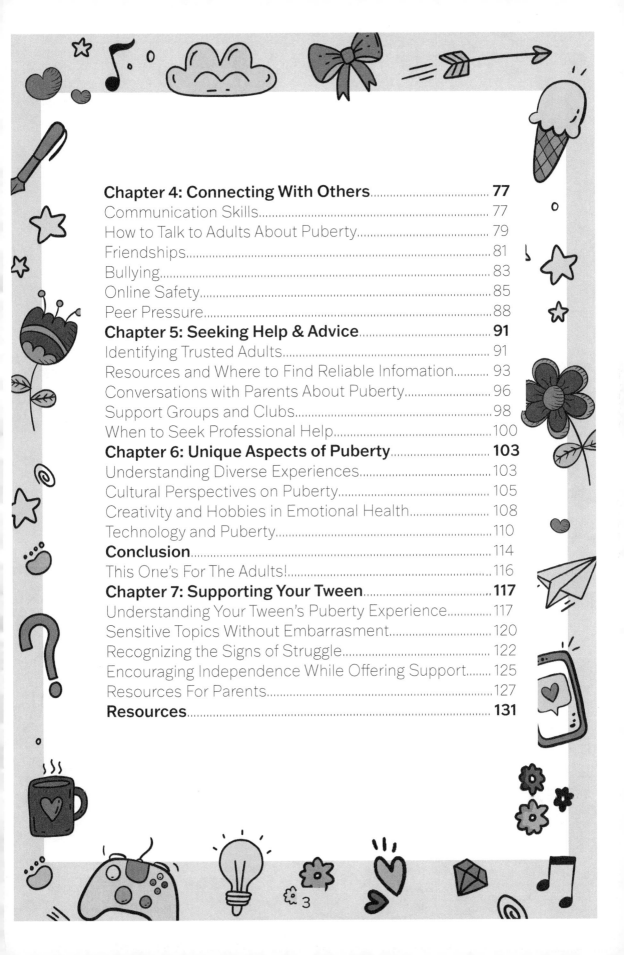

INTRODUCTION

Hey there! So, you've probably noticed that life's about to hand you a one-way ticket to the wild ride known as puberty. Buckle up, because it's not just any journey—it's a whirlwind adventure of growth, self-discovery, and, let's be honest, some pretty weird and wonderful changes. Think of it less like an awkward phase (even though, yes, there will be moments) and more like unlocking the next level of the amazing game of "you."

Now, why am I, a grown-up, dabbling in the mysteries of tween life? Well, because I've been there, done that, and got the T-shirt (which, admittedly, might not fit anymore). But beyond my own rollercoaster ride through puberty, I've spent years working with awesome kids like you, diving deep into the world of adolescent development, and collecting stories and wisdom like they're going out of style. My mission? To be the guide I wish I had when I was your age, offering you a mix of empathy, understanding, and some pretty handy tips to navigate this whole puberty thing.

This book isn't just about the nitty-gritty of growing pains, though. Sure, we'll chat about the physical stuff—breasts, periods, body odor (oh my!)—but we're also going to explore the emotional rollercoasters and the social mazes. It's a holistic look at this whole growing-up biz, because you're not just a walking puberty encyclopedia entry—you're a whole, complex person dealing with a whole lot of new stuff.

And let's get one thing straight: this puberty gig doesn't look the same for everyone. Nope. It's as unique as you are, and that's pretty darn special.

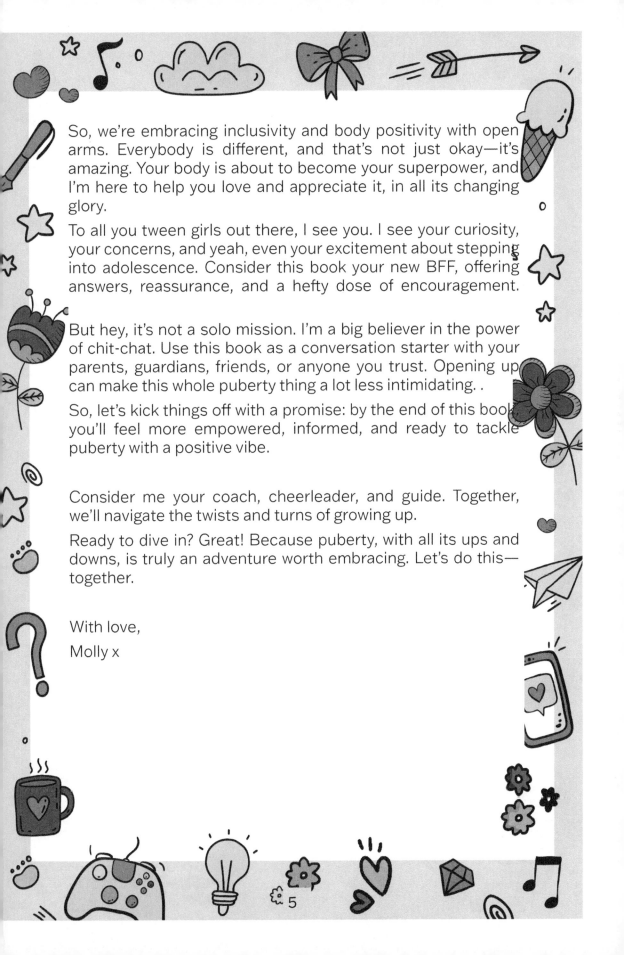

So, we're embracing inclusivity and body positivity with open arms. Everybody is different, and that's not just okay—it's amazing. Your body is about to become your superpower, and I'm here to help you love and appreciate it, in all its changing glory.

To all you tween girls out there, I see you. I see your curiosity, your concerns, and yeah, even your excitement about stepping into adolescence. Consider this book your new BFF, offering answers, reassurance, and a hefty dose of encouragement.

But hey, it's not a solo mission. I'm a big believer in the power of chit-chat. Use this book as a conversation starter with your parents, guardians, friends, or anyone you trust. Opening up can make this whole puberty thing a lot less intimidating. .

So, let's kick things off with a promise: by the end of this book, you'll feel more empowered, informed, and ready to tackle puberty with a positive vibe.

Consider me your coach, cheerleader, and guide. Together, we'll navigate the twists and turns of growing up.

Ready to dive in? Great! Because puberty, with all its ups and downs, is truly an adventure worth embracing. Let's do this—together.

With love,

Molly x

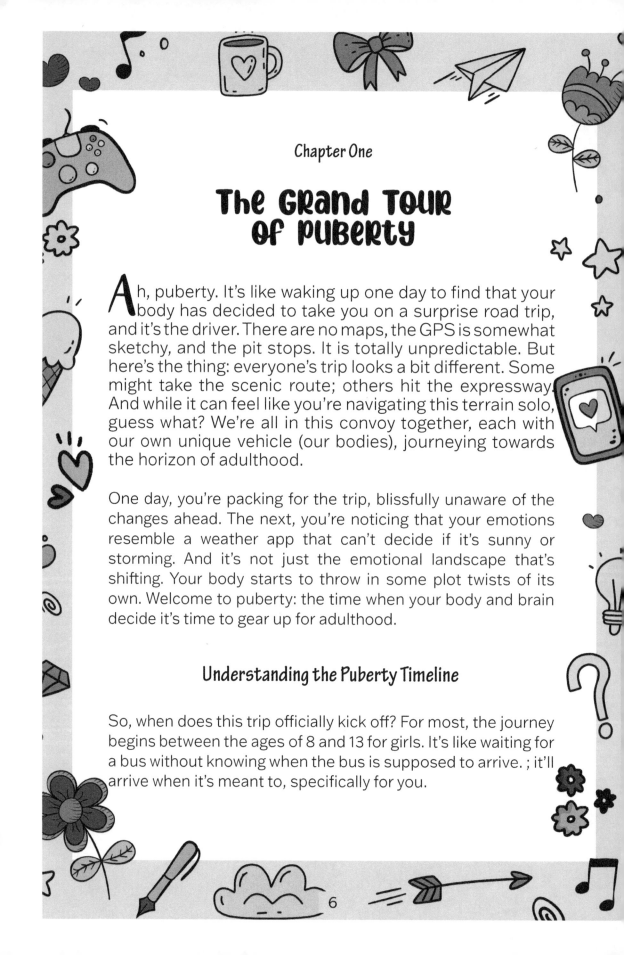

Chapter One

The Grand Tour of Puberty

Ah, puberty. It's like waking up one day to find that your body has decided to take you on a surprise road trip, and it's the driver. There are no maps, the GPS is somewhat sketchy, and the pit stops. It is totally unpredictable. But here's the thing: everyone's trip looks a bit different. Some might take the scenic route; others hit the expressway. And while it can feel like you're navigating this terrain solo, guess what? We're all in this convoy together, each with our own unique vehicle (our bodies), journeying towards the horizon of adulthood.

One day, you're packing for the trip, blissfully unaware of the changes ahead. The next, you're noticing that your emotions resemble a weather app that can't decide if it's sunny or storming. And it's not just the emotional landscape that's shifting. Your body starts to throw in some plot twists of its own. Welcome to puberty: the time when your body and brain decide it's time to gear up for adulthood.

Understanding the Puberty Timeline

So, when does this trip officially kick off? For most, the journey begins between the ages of 8 and 13 for girls. It's like waiting for a bus without knowing when the bus is supposed to arrive. ; it'll arrive when it's meant to, specifically for you.

This phase, my friends, is where your body starts laying the groundwork for all the growth and changes you're about to experience. It's preparing to build you up, quite literally, from the inside out.

But here's where it gets interesting: no two trips are identical. You might notice some friends starting their journey earlier or later than you, and that's perfectly okay. It's all down to a magical thing called genetics. Yep, the same reason you might have your mom's eyes or your dad's laugh plays a big role in determining when your puberty journey kicks off. Your genetic blueprint, which you've had since day one, has a schedule all its own.

Now, let's talk about what you can expect to see on this journey. First up, we have physical changes. This is where your body starts to change into its adult form. Think of it like a caterpillar transforming into a butterfly, except instead of wings, you get curves, and rather than emerging overnight, it takes a few years. You'll grow taller, your hips might widen, and yes, boobs start to develop. It's like your body is sculpting or reinventing itself, adding and adjusting, getting you ready for the grand reveal.

But puberty isn't just a physical journey; it's an emotional rollercoaster, too. One minute, you're laughing; the next, you're crying over a commercial. It's all thanks to the hormonal cocktail being mixed up in your body. Hormones are the chemical messengers zipping around your body, dictating all these changes. And while they're incredibly good at their job, they can make things feel pretty intense.

Variability is Normal

Remember how we said everyone's journey is unique? Well, that's because puberty doesn't follow a one-size-fits-all timetable. Some might sprint through the changes, while others take their time. And no matter where you find yourself on this spectrum, it's normal. There's no deadline you need to meet or a box you have to fit into. This trip is yours, and yours alone, and it unfolds at just the right pace for you.

The role of genetics in all of this can't be overstated. It's like having a secret code inside you that determines not just when you'll start this journey but also how you'll navigate it. If your family tree shows a pattern of people who hit puberty early, , chances are, you might hit puberty early, too. On the flip side, if the women in your family tended to start puberty later, you might find yourself in the same boat. It's all written in your DNA, the unique script of you.

And while genetics plays a starring role, it's not the sole director of this show. Environmental factors, nutrition, and overall health also get a say in when and how puberty will affect you. It's a complex interaction of elements, all coming together to kick-start this next chapter of your life.

As you start this journey, remember that puberty is not a race, nor is it a competition. It's a natural process, a sign that your body is doing exactly what it's supposed to do at exactly the right time for you. So, as you start to notice these changes, both physical and emotional, know that you're not alone. We're all part of this grand tour, each with our own unique itinerary, discovering what it means to grow up. And while the road may be unpredictable, it's also incredibly exciting. Welcome to puberty, the adventure of a lifetime.

For those of you wanting to chat to your mom, aunt or older sisters about puberty but not knowing where to start- For many it can feel really awkward! A good conversation opener may simply be, "Do you remember the first time you got your period? How old were you?" This could give you an indication as to what your genetic line up may be, it can also be a great way to ease into the topic.

Why Everyone's Puberty Experience Is Different

When each girl's puberty experience starts, it's like every person is handed a custom-made map at the start. No two maps are the same because no two people are the same. Every girl is made in her own unique way. This uniqueness is shaped by a variety of factors.

Individual differences: Imagine your body as a complex machine. Just as every machine has its quirks, so does your body. Genetics loads the dice, setting the stage for when and how puberty unfolds. But it's not just about the genes. Your environment - from the air you breathe to the water you drink, and even the stress levels you experience - plays a supporting role. Then there's health. Nutritional intake, physical activity, and even sleep patterns can accelerate or put the brakes on puberty's onset. It's like a dance where genetics leads, but environment and health definitely get a say in the steps.

Cultural perspectives: Now, step back and look at the bigger picture. Across the globe, cultures have their own ways of recognizing and celebrating this transition from being a child into becoming a full-grown adult. Some cultures throw parties, others have ceremonies, and a few might not acknowledge puberty much at all.

These cultural nuances do more than mark the occasion; they shape how individuals feel about the changes they're undergoing. Growing up in a culture that celebrates puberty might make you more excited about the changes, whereas in cultures where it's not openly discussed, you might feel more anxious, scared or even make you feel secretive about the things your body is going through. Be forewarned that at certain times you might even feel ashamed of your body because of all of the changes that are taking place inside you.

Impact of early or late onset: Timing matters, but not in the way you might think. Being an early bloomer or a latecomer has its pros and cons. Early bloomers get a head start, but they also might feel self-conscious, towering over or developing faster than their peers. Late bloomers, on the other hand, might feel left behind, watching their friends change while they wait for their turn. Both scenarios can feel isolating, but they also offer unique perspectives. Early bloomers learn to navigate their new reality sooner, while late bloomers might develop patience and understanding watching their peers go first.

Embracing your journey: Here's the heart of the matter. Your puberty experience, with its timing, symptoms, and annoyances, is yours alone. And while it's easy to fall into the comparison trap, especially with social media constantly showcasing highlights from everyone else's lives, it's crucial to remember that your journey is valid. Your feelings are valid, too. Embracing this phase, with all its ups and downs, is a form of self-love. It's about recognizing that, like a snowflake, your experience is unique and beautiful in its complexity.

So, as you navigate this period of your life, remember, it's not about keeping pace with others but honoring your own timing and experiences. Whether you're the first in your friend group to need a bra or the last one to have a growth spurt, your journey is unfolding exactly as it should for you. And among all the changes, creating a sense of self-compassion and embracing your individual journey can transform this phase from something to endure into something to celebrate.

The Science Behind Puberty: Hormones and How They Affect You

Imagine your body as a busy city, and hormones are the messengers zipping around, ensuring that everything runs smoothly. These chemical messengers are critical for initiating and regulating the vast array of changes during puberty. They're like the directors of a movie, guiding the development of the plot (your growth) and influencing the emotional soundtrack of your day-to-day life.

Introduction to Hormones

Hormones are substances produced by your body's glands and released into the bloodstream, where they travel to target organs and tissues, delivering instructions that help regulate your body's growth, metabolism, and reproductive processes. Think of them as the body's communication system, sending signals to keep everything in balance.

Key Players

Among the cast of hormonal characters, a few standouts play leading roles in the puberty story:

Estrogen: This hormone kicks off the development of female physical features, such as boobs and wider hips. It's like the architect designing the changes that transform the body.

Testosterone: While it's often associated with males, testosterone is also present in females, where it influences muscle growth, bone density, and even the mood music playing in the background of your day.

Growth Hormones: These are the builders, responsible for those sudden height increases and the growth spurt that's a hallmark of puberty.They're working overtime, constructing the adult version of you.

Thyroid Hormones: Think of these as the regulators, ensuring that your energy levels and metabolism keep pace with the rapid changes happening in your body.

Emotional Effects of Hormones

Now, for the plot twist: as these hormones flood your system, they don't just remodel your physical appearance; they also stir up the emotional landscape. One moment, you might feel on top of the world, and the next, a TV commercial could have you crying. . It's all due to the hormonal roller coaster that is subtly influencing your brain's chemistry, affecting how you feel and how you look at the world around you.

Picture estrogen and testosterone not just as physical architects but as DJs at the control panel of your emotions, mixing tracks that can set your mood swinging from one extreme to another. This emotional remix is a natural part of puberty, as your body adjusts to its new hormonal balance.

Maintaining Hormonal Balance

Given the key role hormones play, keeping them in harmony is like making sure all the instruments in an orchestra are in tune

Here are some lifestyle tips that hit the right notes for supporting hormonal balance:

Nutritious diet: Give your body energy with a variety of foods rich in vitamins and minerals supports hormone production and regulation. Think of colorful fruits and vegetables, whole grains, and lean proteins as the essential playlist for a healthy hormonal balance.

Regular exercise: Physical activity isn't just good for your muscles and heart; it also plays a tune that encourages hormonal harmony.

Activities like swimming, biking, or even dancing in your room can help reduce stress and promote a healthy endocrine system.

Adequate sleep: Catching enough Z's is like hitting the refresh button for your body and mind. During sleep, your body gets to work repairing, growing, and rebalancing hormones. Aim for 8-10, even 12 hours a night to give your body the downtime it needs.

Stress management: Chronic stress can throw your hormonal symphony out of whack, leading to a big number of emotional ups and downs. Techniques like deep breathing, journaling, or practicing mindfulness are like tuning the instruments of your mind and body, helping to keep your hormones—and by extension, your emotions—in check.

Navigating puberty with an understanding of the hormonal changes at play can demystify many of the experiences you're going through. It's like having a backstage pass to your own development, offering insights into the physical and emotional transformations unfolding.

With this knowledge, you're better equipped to ride the waves of puberty, understanding that the ups and downs are part of a natural process. And remember, you're not alone. Everyone going through puberty is part of the same concert, each playing their unique tune, contributing to the symphony of growing up.

Decoding Your Growth Spurts: Height, Weight, and Body Shape Changes

During this stage of life, your body goes through a series of rapid transformations, akin to a caterpillar metamorphosing into a butterfly. It's a period of accelerated growth, not just in height but across various physical dimensions, marking the transition from childhood into adolescence.

What to Expect

Height Spurts: Suddenly finding that your favorite jeans have turned into ankle-grazers overnight? That's your first sign of a growth spurt. Typically, girls experience this surge in height around the ages of 10 to 14. It's like your body hits the fast-forward button, growing 2 to 3 inches (5 to 7.5 cm) or more in a year.

Weight Changes: Along with getting taller, you'll notice your weight going up. This is perfectly normal and necessary, as your body accumulates fat in preparation for potential future growth and development. It's laying down the foundations for the adult you.

Body Shape Transformations: This is where things get interesting. Your body starts to change shape, developing curves where there were none before. Your hips widen, preparing for the possibility of childbirth in the far future, and fat distribution changes, marking the blueprint of your adult body shape.

Nutrition's Role

Imagine your body is a high-performance vehicle. Just as a car needs the right fuel to run efficiently, your body needs a balanced mix of nutrients to support the rapid growth happening during puberty. **Here's a quick breakdown:**

Protein: The building block of your muscles and tissues. Including protein in your diet ensures that your body has the necessary materials for growth.

Calcium and Vitamin D: These two work hand in hand to strengthen your bones. With the significant growth in height during puberty, ensuring your bones are strong is crucial.

Iron: Especially important for girls, . Iron supports healthy blood circulation and can help prevent tiredness. You may not have known that being constantly tired is a common issue during rapid growth phases.

Body Image and Self-Esteem

As your body changes and shifts, it's natural to check out these changes, comparing them to your peers or the often unrealistic, standards set by social media. These observations can lead to feelings of inadequacy or discomfort with your changing body, impacting self-esteem.

Here are a few strategies to maintain a positive body image:

Focus on Functionality: Remember, your body is capable of incredible things. Whether it's running, dancing, or simply breathing, appreciating what your body can do helps shift focus from appearance to appreciation.

Limit Comparison: It's easy to fall into the trap of comparing your body to others', but it's as productive as comparing apples and oranges. Remember, diversity in body shapes and sizes is what makes us uniquely beautiful.

Positive Affirmations: Practice speaking kindly to yourself. Positive affirmations can reinforce self-love and acceptance. Saying simple phrases like , "I am strong. I am capable. I am enough." can go a long way in improving your self-esteem.

When to Seek Advice

While most changes during puberty are a normal part of development, there are times when it might be necessary to consult a doctor.

Here are a few signs to watch out for:

Delayed or Early Growth: If you notice that your growth spurt is significantly earlier or later than your peers, it might be worth discussing with a doctor. While a broad range of normal exists, extreme differences might require a check-up.

Disproportionate Growth: If certain parts of your body are growing more rapidly or slowly compared to the rest, or if you experience pain associated with growth, seeking medical advice is a good idea.

Nutritional Concerns: Struggles with eating, whether it's under-eating or overeating, can affect your growth and development. If you have concerns about your diet or nutrition, a healthcare provider can offer guidance.

Navigating puberty is like learning how to steer a boat through uncharted waters. Each day brings a new discovery about your body and yourself. Remember, these transformations, as confusing as they may seem, are your body's way of changing you into the adult you're becoming. With a balanced diet, a healthy dose of self-love, and the occasional check-in with doctors when needed, you're well-equipped to embrace these changes with confidence and grace.

Breast Development: Sizes, Shapes, and Self-Exams

Moving along this path of growth and transformation, let's shift focus to a topic that often comes with a mix of anticipation and a dash of anxiety for many girls: breast development. This stage of puberty can feel like you've hit a fast-forward button, with changes that are as unique as your fingerprint. It's a time when understanding and embracing the diversity of the human body becomes important

Normal Variability

First off, let's set the record straight: when it comes to breasts, there's a vast degree of what is normal for girls. From size and shape to the timing of development, boobs are as diverse as we women are. Some might notice their boobs begin to develop as early as eight years old, while others might not see changes until their mid-teens. And once they start growing, boobs can be many different shapes such as round, oval, asymmetrical, or anywhere in between. This variability isn't just normal; it's expected. So, if you find yourself comparing your body to others', remember, diversity is nature's design, ensuring that no two girls are exactly alike.

Stages of Development

Boob development during puberty follows a series of stages, often referred to as Tanner stages, ranging from stage one (pre-puberty) to stage five (full maturity). It kicks off with the breast bud stage, where you might notice small, tender lumps under one or both nipples. This is your body starting the groundwork for future boob growth. Gradually, these buds grow, develop into actual breast tissue, and eventually take on a more rounded shape. The journey from the first bud to full development can take several years, with each stage unfolding at its own pace. Do not be hard on yourself or compare yourself to your other girl friends. You are not developing too slowly or too fast. You're developing boobs at the exact rate that you're supposed to.

Introduction to Self-Exams

As your boobs develop, getting into the habit of regular self-exams is a smart move. These exams are not just about monitoring growth; they're a proactive way to check for any unusual changes or lumps. Starting in your teen years, you can dedicate a few minutes each month to give yourself a self-exam. Doing so can set the foundation for lifelong breast health. What is the ideal time to give yourself breast exams?

The ideal time to give yourself breast exams is about a week after your period ends, when breasts are least likely to be tender or swollen. You might be sitting there thinking: "Ok this information is strange, yet kind of intriguing. How in the world will I know the best time to give myself a boob examination? Here is what you do: You use a gentle, circular motion with your fingers and palms of your hands to feel for any lumps, thickening, or changes, covering both the breasts and underarm areas. Remember, finding something unfamiliar isn't a cause for immediate concern, but a sign to reach out to your doctor for further evaluation.

Dealing with Discomfort

As boobs begin their growth spurt, discomfort and tenderness can tag along. This sensitivity is your body's response to the hormonal changes that are steering puberty. For some, it's a mild inconvenience; for others, it can be more intense and painful.

If you're finding breast tenderness a bit too bothersome, here are a few tips to ease the discomfort:

Right Bra Matters: A well-fitting, supportive bra can be a game-changer, especially during sports or other physical activities. Look for bras with soft, stretchy fabric that provide support without squeezing your breasts too tight. And remember, your bra size will change as you grow, so getting measured every once in a while, can reassure you're always wearing the right size bra. Find a bra that fits your body and your lifestyle.

Gentle Care: During times of heightened breast sensitivity, opting for gentle, unscented body products can help avoid further irritation. Similarly, soft, breathable fabrics can keep discomfort away, letting your skin breathe.

Warm Compresses: For moments when tenderness feels more intense, applying a warm compress can offer some relief. It's a simple, soothing remedy that can ease the discomfort.

Navigating boob development is a significant part of growing up.. It's a time of becoming familiar with your body's changes, learning to care for it, and most importantly, developing a relationship with yourself. You'll want to start and keep a relationship with yourself that is rooted in kindness and acceptance. Whether you're figuring out the annoyance of bra sizes, exploring the stages of boob development, or getting the hang of self-exams, remember, this phase is just one part of the broader tapestry of growth during puberty. Each change, each new development, is a step towards the person you're becoming, and learning to embrace each change with understanding and care can transform this time of transition into a journey of empowerment.

The Lowdown on Body Hair

Managing New Growth

With puberty's arrival, your body kicks into high gear, sprouting hair in new and unexpected places. This fuzz phenomenon isn't just about swapping the smoothness of childhood for the textured terrain of adolescence; it's a sign that your body's ecosystems are evolving, responding to the hormonal shifts that define this period of growth. Understanding why and how this happens, along with navigating the sea of choices regarding body hair, offers a fresh perspective on a topic often shrouded in whispers and giggles.

Understanding New Hair Growth

So, why does hair start to appear where it once didn't? It all circles back to those hormonal messengers at play during puberty, particularly testosterone. Yes, even in females, testosterone dictates the hair growth soundtrack It turns up the volume in areas of your body like underarms, legs, and the pubic region.

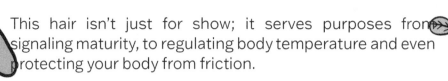

This hair isn't just for show; it serves purposes from signaling maturity, to regulating body temperature and even protecting your body from friction.

Seeing hair sprout in new spots can feel like your body's pulling a fast one on you, but it's all part of the plan, a natural element of the growth mixtape your body's been curating since day one. You don't need to be afraid of it. If you're struggling with it, ask a trusted family member or your doctor about it. Get all of those burning questions answered.

Choices in Hair Management

When it comes to dealing with this newfound hair, the landscape is as different as the individuals navigating it. Here's where personal choice takes center stage, shining a spotlight on the fact that there's no right or wrong way to manage your body hair. Options for hair management range widely, from letting nature take its course to exploring removal methods like shaving, waxing, or using hair removal creams. Each choice comes with its own set of rules and considerations, from the maintenance involved to how your skin reacts to different methods.

Shaving: This is a common first step for many girls. It offers a quick, cost-effective method to remove hair. It requires a steady hand and understanding the importance of using a clean, sharp razor to minimize nicks and irritation. Ask your mom or older sibling to teach you how to use a razor to shave your legs for the first time. Remember, there is no shame in asking questions or in asking for help.

Waxing: This technique provides longer-lasting results by removing hair from the root but it can be more painful and costly. If you've found out that you have a low threshold for pain, this may not be the best option for you. It's often done professionally, though at-home kits are available.

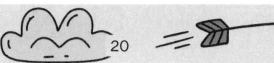

Hair Removal Creams: These creams are chemical-based products that dissolve hair just below the skin's surface. While they may be convenient for you, it's important to test your skin for sensitivity and follow instructions closely to avoid any nasty chemical burns.

Natural Methods: For those girls who are leaning towards a more natural approach, there are options like sugaring which offer a gentler alternative to traditional hair removal methods. Sugaring uses simple ingredients like sugar, water, and lemon juice.

Remember, managing body hair is your call. It's about what makes you feel the most comfortable and confident in your skin. It's never about bending to peer pressure or societies expectations.

Safety First

For those opting to remove body hair, doing so safely is key. Each method, from shaving to waxing, comes with its own playbook for minimizing risks and ensuring a smooth process:

Shaving: Always use a clean, sharp blade and consider applying a shaving gel or cream to protect your skin. Shave in the direction of hair growth to reduce irritation.

Waxing: Whether at home or in a salon, ensure the wax is not too hot in order to prevent burns. Following post-wax care instructions can help soothe the skin and avoid ingrown hairs.

Hair Removal Creams: Do a patch test before full applying each hair removal cream that you decide to try. You can do this to check for any bad or even allergic reactions. Using these creams in well-ventilated areas is also wise to avoid inhaling fumes.

Natural Methods: Even with natural solutions like sugaring, skin sensitivity can be an issue. Test on a small area of your skin first and follow up with a soothing moisturizer to calm the skin.

In the grand scheme of puberty, body hair is but one thread among many, a natural part of the body's evolution. How you choose to deal with it—embracing, altering, or removing—is a personal decision. It is also one that offers another way to express your individuality and allows you to exercise control over your body. As you navigate these choices, remember, the most important opinion on your body hair is your own, a reflection of your comfort, beliefs, and values.

Skin Changes: Tackling Acne with Confidence

Navigating the seas of puberty brings about a variety of changes, not just beneath the surface, but quite literally on the surface of your skin. It's as if overnight, your skin decides it's time to mix things up, leading to one of puberty's most talked-about landmarks: acne. But why does acne become your uninvited guest during these years, and how can you manage it without letting it dampen your spirits? Let's peel back the layers.

Why Acne Happens

Acne, in its essence, is your skin throwing a bit of a tantrum, thanks mainly to a surge in hormones known as androgens. These hormones kick oil production into high gear, leading to clogged pores which, in turn, become the perfect party spots for bacteria. The result? Blackheads, whiteheads, and those oh not-so-joyful pimples. It's like your skin is putting on its own unpredictable show, and everyone's experience in the audience is a bit different.One crucial thing to remember is that acne isn't a sign that

One important thing to remember is that acne isn't a sign that you're doing anything wrong. It's a natural part of growing up, and it's a rite of passage that most people will experience to some degree. It's also not a one-size-fits-all situation; while some might get the occasional pimple, others might find themselves dealing with more persistent forms of acne. And while genetics play a role in determining your skin's script during puberty, lifestyle factors also have their parts to play.

Effective Skincare Routines

When it comes to managing acne, establishing a skincare routine that's as unique as you are is key.

Here's a basic outline, adaptable to fit your skin's needs:

Gentle Cleansing: Starting and ending your day with a gentle cleanser can help keep your skin's oil levels balanced and reduce the likelihood of clogged pores. Look for products labeled "non-comedogenic," meaning they're designed not to block pores.

Moisturizing: It might seem nonproductive to add moisture to acne-prone skin. However, hydrating helps maintain your skin's natural barrier. You can find lightweight, oil-free moisturizers that hydrate without adding extra oil to your skin.

Sun Protection: Acne treatments can make your skin more sensitive to the sun, so applying a broad-spectrum sunscreen daily is important..Again, skin care moisturizers that do not block your pores are your best bet.

Spot Treatments: For those pesky pimples, spot treatments containing benzoyl peroxide or salicylic acid can be effective. They're like targeted mini warriors, going straight to the source to combat bacteria and reduce inflammation.

Customizing this routine to fit your skin type—oily, dry, combination, or sensitive—assures you that you're providing your skin with what it needs, nothing more, and nothing less. And remember, consistency is your friend; giving your routine time to work its magic is part of the process.

Debunking Acne Myths

With acne comes a plethora of myths, tales as old as time that somehow still find their way into our beliefs. Let's set the record straight on a few:

"Eating greasy food causes acne." While a well-balanced diet is important for overall health, there's no direct link between that slice of pizza and a breakout. It's more about how your skin reacts to an internal hormonal dance than what you're eating.

"Acne is a sign of dirty skin." Acne has more to do with oil production and hormonal fluctuations than cleanliness. Over-washing or scrubbing your skin too hard can actually irritate your skin more and worsen acne.

"Popping pimples will make them go away faster." This is a ticket to Scarsville. Popping pimples can push bacteria deeper into the skin, leading to more inflammation and even scarring.

By leaning on facts rather than myths, you empower yourself to take better care of your skin, making informed choices that support its health and improve your confidence.

Seeking Professional Help

Sometimes, despite your best efforts, acne decides to stick around, or it becomes too severe to manage with over-the-counter products alone. That's when bringing in the pros—a dermatologist, also known as a skin doctor—can make all the difference. If you find your acne is significantly affecting your self-esteem, causing physical discomfort, or leaving scars, it's time to seek the dermatologist's expert advice.

A dermatologist can provide a specific treatment plan for your skin, potentially including prescription medications. They can also offer insights into lifestyle changes or products that might help keep breakouts away .

Remember, reaching out for help isn't a sign of weakness or defeat. It's a great step towards understanding and taking care of your skin. Acne, after all, is just one part of the puberty experience, and with the right tools and knowledge at your disposal, it's one you can navigate with confidence and clarity.

Your First Period: What It Is and How to Prepare

In the midst of all the changes puberty throws at you, getting your first period stands out as a major milestone. Some call it "Aunt Flo's visit," others refer to it as "riding the crimson wave," but technically, it's known as menstruation. It's your body's natural way of shedding the lining of the uterus when there isn't a pregnancy. This cycle is a key part of the reproductive system, preparing your body each month for the possibility of pregnancy, also known as having a baby.

Now, let's break down what you can do to feel ready and less like you're navigating a mystery.

Getting Ready for the Big Day

The timing of your first period can feel like waiting for a surprise guest to show up—you know they're coming, but you're not quite sure when. Most girls get their period between the ages of 12 and 14, but anywhere from ages eight to 16 is within the normal range.

Here's how you can prep:

Stay stocked: Keep a few pads or tampons on hand, whether in your backpack, locker, or in your bathroom at home. This way, you're not caught off guard whenever your period starts.

Know the signs: Your body might send you signals that your period is on its way. Some girls experience bloating, mood swings, or cramps in the days leading up to it. If you notice these changes, it might be time to make sure you're prepared. You can also prepare by taking over the counter medications such as ibuprofen once or twice per day to alleviate the pain that is caused by PMS, also known as the premenstrual cycle.

Chat it out: Talk to someone you trust about what to expect when your first period comes on—whether you talk to a parent, older sibling, or friend.. Sharing experiences can offer comfort and practical advice.

Choosing Menstrual Products

When it comes to managing your period, there's a variety of products out there to choose from, each product comes with its own set of pros and cons.

Here's a quick overview:

Pads: Often the go-to for first-timers, pads are worn inside your underwear and come in various thicknesses and lengths. They're easy to use and great for overnight protection.

Tampons: These are inserted into the vagina to absorb period blood flow. They come with or without applicators and in different absorbances. If you're active or want to swim during your period, tampons are a great choice.

Menstrual cups: : A reusable option, cups are inserted into the vagina where they catch the blood from your period. . They can be worn for up to 12 hours, making them eco-friendly and cost-effective over time.

Period underwear: These look and feel like regular underwear but have a special layer to absorb menstrual flow. They're reusable and can be a good backup for other products or used alone on light days.

It might take some experimenting to find what works best for you, and that's perfectly normal. What's important is choosing products that fit your lifestyle and comfort level.

Navigating Symptoms

While some girls breeze through their periods with barely a hiccup, others might experience symptoms like cramps, which can range from mildly annoying to seriously ouch-worthy.

Here are some ways to ease the discomfort:

Heat therapy: Applying a warm heating pad or hot water bottle to your lower abdomen can relax the muscles and ease cramps.

Stay hydrated: Drinking plenty of water can help reduce bloating and ease discomfort. It sounds simple, but it works wonders.

Exercise: Light exercise, like walking or yoga, can release endorphins, your body's natural painkillers, and help alleviate cramps.

Over-the-counter relief: If cramps are making your day miserable, over-the-counter pain relievers like ibuprofen can offer relief. Just be sure to follow the dosage instructions or talk with a doctor if you're not sure of what medicine to take.

For symptoms that seem out of the ordinary or too tough to handle, reaching out to a doctor is a smart move. They can offer personalized advice and solutions to make your period more manageable.

Getting your first period is a sign that your body is working just as it should, embarking on a cycle that's a normal part of being female. While it might seem daunting and intimidating at first, with a bit of preparation and understanding, you can navigate this new phase with confidence. Remember, every woman's experience with getting their period is as unique as she is, and there's no "right" way to feel about it.

Whether you greet your first period with excitement, indifference, or a mix of emotions, what matters most is arming yourself with knowledge and support so you can face this change head-on

Understanding Your Reproductive System: A Guide for Tweens

Anatomy 101

Your body is an incredible piece of biological machinery, and part of what makes it so fascinating is the reproductive system. Think of it as a highly specialized ecosystem designed for one of the most miraculous functions – the potential to create life. The main parts of the female reproductive system include the ovaries, fallopian tubes, uterus, cervix, and vagina.

Each plays a pivotal role, from the ovaries that store your eggs and release them during ovulation, to the uterus where a fertilized egg can develop into a baby. It's like a beautifully orchestrated sequence, where every component has its unique function, working together in harmony.

The Menstrual Cycle Demystified

Now, onto your period , a topic often shrouded in mystery and confusion. Breaking it down, the cycle can be divided into several phases, starting with menstruation or the shedding of the lining of your uterus. Menstruation is when the lining of the uterus thickens up in preparation for a potential pregnancy. Then the lining is shed if no fertilized egg has implanted into your uterus. Following menstruation, the body enters the follicular phase, where the ovaries prepare an egg for release.

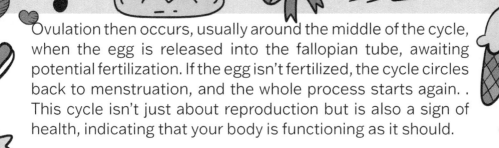

Ovulation then occurs, usually around the middle of the cycle, when the egg is released into the fallopian tube, awaiting potential fertilization. If the egg isn't fertilized, the cycle circles back to menstruation, and the whole process starts again. . This cycle isn't just about reproduction but is also a sign of health, indicating that your body is functioning as it should.

Respecting and Caring for Your Body

Understanding your reproductive system brings a responsibility to care for it. Hygiene is important.; You can do simple practices like changing pads or tampons regularly during your period, keeping the genital area clean, and wearing breathable fabrics which can promote your reproductive health. Regular health check-ups, even if everything seems fine, are key to catching and addressing any issues early. Listening to your body's signals is equally important. . If something feels off, whether it's unusual pain, changes in your period, or discomfort during your period, it's important to speak up and seek advice from a doctor. Your body communicates with you in various ways, and tuning into these signals can help you maintain not just reproductive health but overall well-being.

Privacy and Boundaries

Lastly, in a world where information is at our fingertips, and discussions about health are becoming more open, setting boundaries around your body and health is vital. Privacy concerning your reproductive health is a personal right. Deciding who you share information with, whether it's parents, doctors, or friends, should be a choice that feels comfortable for you. It's okay to seek advice and share concerns, but it's also okay to keep certain information private if that's what you prefer. Finding a balance between openness and privacy, especially regarding something as personal as reproductive health, is a personal journey. Respecting your comfort level, and the boundaries of others, fosters a healthy environment for discussions about these important topics.

The Emotional Rollercoaster: Navigating Mood Swings

Navigating puberty isn't just about physical changes; it's equally about the whirlwind of emotions that can sweep you up without a moment's notice. You might find yourself laughing at a joke one minute and tearing up over it the next. These mood swings, as wild and unpredictable as they are, come from the hormonal fluctuations that are the engine of puberty.

Why Emotions Fluctuate

Imagine your hormones as a team of DJs, each taking turns at the decks, playing a mix of tunes that can take your feelings from one extreme to another. These hormonal changes are directly linked to the emotional highs and lows that you experience while on your period. Estrogen and testosterone, in particular, don't just work on your body; they also have a dance with your brain, impacting how you feel and respond to the world around you.

Coping Strategies

Riding this emotional rollercoaster with a bit of finesse involves having a toolkit at your disposal.

Here are some strategies that can help smooth out the bumps:

Mindfulness: This practice involves staying present and fully experiencing the moment without judgment. Simple mindfulness exercises like deep breathing or focusing on the sensations in your body can act as an anchor, bringing you back to calm when emotions run high.

Journaling: Keeping a journal offers a private space to express your thoughts and feelings. It's like having a conversation with yourself on paper, helping to process emotions and often offering new perspectives on why you feel the way you do.

Talking to Trusted Individuals: Sometimes, sharing what you're going through with someone you trust can be incredibly relieving. Whether it's a parent, friend, or teacher, talking about your feelings can lighten your emotional load. The person you're confiding in can provide some much-needed support and advice.

When Emotions Seem Overwhelming

There are moments when your feelings might feel like they're too much to handle alone. Recognizing when it's time to seek help is important.

Here are some signs that it might be time to reach out:

Persistent Sadness or Anxiety: If you find yourself feeling down or anxious most of the time, and if you find that you are unable to shake off these feelings.

Changes in Sleep or Appetite: If you ever find yourself losing interest in hobbies or activities that used to bring you joy.

Withdrawal from Activities You Enjoy: Losing interest in hobbies or activities that used to bring you joy.

Difficulty Concentrating: If you ever find it hard to focus on schoolwork or daily tasks.

If any of these resonate with you, talking to a trusted adult or seeking professional help can offer the support you need to navigate these feelings. Remember, reaching out is a sign of strength, not weakness. It's about taking care of your emotional well-being with the same attention you give to your physical health.

Building Emotional Resilience

Developing emotional resilience and strength is like strengthening a muscle; it takes practice and patience.

Here are some ways to foster resilience during the ups and downs of puberty:

Positive Relationships: Surround yourself with supportive friends and family. Supportive people can provide a nurturing environment that bolsters your emotional strength.

Setting Realistic Goals: Achieving small, manageable goals can boost your confidence and sense of accomplishment, reinforcing that you can overcome challenges.

Self-Care: Regularly engage in activities that promote well-being, such as exercise, reading, or spending time in nature. All of those activities can enhance your mood and resilience.

Accepting Change: Recognize that change is a part of life and learning to adapt can decrease the stress and anxiety that you feel when it's associated with the unknown mysteries of life.

Building emotional resilience doesn't happen overnight. It's a process of learning, growing, and adapting. With each challenge faced and overcome, you gain the strength and wisdom to handle the next, moving through puberty not just with endurance but with an understanding and appreciation for the complexity of your emotions.

Chapter Two

GLOWING THROUGH PUBERTY

Imagine you're an artist, and your skin is the canvas. Puberty, then, is like being handed a whole new set of paints—some bright, some a bit muddled. It's up to you to learn the best ways to use them, blending and balancing until you find that perfect harmony. Your skin, after all, is going to be with you through thick and thin, so why not make it a masterpiece of self-care and confidence?

Navigating the skincare aisle can feel like decoding a complex puzzle. With shelves packed full of products screaming "Use me!" it's easy to feel overwhelmed. But here's the secret: mastering your skincare routine isn't about having more products; it's about having the right ones and using them well. Let's break it down, step by step, to build a skincare routine that feels like a warm hug to your skin.

Creating a Skincare Routine That Works For You

So, when does this trip officially kick off? For most, the journey begins between the ages of 8 and 13 for girls. It's like waiting for a bus without a timetable; it'll arrive when it's meant to specifically for you.

Oily: Your skin often has a shine, and you might find yourself reaching for blotting papers or powder throughout the day.

Dry: Your skin can feel tight, especially after washing it, and flaky patches aren't strangers to you.

Combination: Some areas (like your nose and forehead) are shiny, while others (such as your cheeks) are dry.

Sensitive: Your skin might react to new products with redness, itching, or breakouts.

Knowing your skin type is like having a roadmap; it guides you to the products that will work best for you, not against you.

Basic Skincare Steps

Now, onto the building blocks of any good skincare routine: cleansing, moisturizing, and applying sunscreen. This trio is your best defense against the elements and the foundation for healthy skin.

Cleansing: Think of it as clearing the canvas. A gentle cleanser removes dirt, oil, and makeup without stripping your skin of moisture and the vitamins it needs on a daily basis. Doing this morning and night keeps your pores happy and your skin clear.

Moisturizing: After cleansing, your skin is like a sponge, ready to soak up some hydration. A moisturizer keeps your skin balanced and prevents it from becoming too dry or oily.

Sunscreen: The sun is the biggest aging factor for skin. A broad-spectrum SPF protects against harmful rays, keeping your skin safe and helping prevent future damage.

Choosing the Right Products

Here's where many get stuck: selecting the right products. With so many options, how do you choose one? Start by reading labels and looking for products formulated for your skin type. Ingredients matter too. For instance, hyaluronic acid is excellent for hydration, while salicylic acid can help unclog pores. If you have sensitive skin, products labeled "fragrance-free" and "for sensitive skin" are your allies. Remember, the price tag on each product doesn't always reflect its effectiveness. Some of the best skincare heroes are budget-friendly and as effective as their high-end counterparts.

Habit Building

Consistency is key. Integrating skincare into your daily routine is like brushing your teeth; it becomes second nature.

Here are a few tips to make skincare a habit everyday:

Set reminders: Until it becomes a routine, setting a reminder on your phone or on a Calander can help keep you on track.

Keep it simple: You're more likely to stick with a routine that's easy to follow. Start with the basics; you can always add steps as you become more comfortable.

Make it fun: Incorporate a little self-pampering into your routine. Play your favorite music or treat yourself to a new face mask as a reward for sticking with it.

Building a skincare routine that works for you doesn't have to be a chore. It's an act of self-care, a way to show love to the skin you're in. As you navigate through puberty, remember that your skin is changing right along with you.

What works today might need adjustment tomorrow, and that's perfectly okay. Skincare is a journey that's personal and unique to you. With the right knowledge and tools at your disposal, you're well on your way to glowing through puberty, armed with confidence and a skincare routine that feels just right.

Period Hygiene: Choosing What's Right for You

Ah, the world of menstrual products! It's like walking into a candy store, but instead of sweets, you're greeted with an array of pads, tampons, cups, and period undies. Each one promises to make your period experience a breeze, but how do you pick? Let's sift through the options, weighing the pros and cons, to find what feels like a high-five for your menstrual cycle.

Overview of Menstrual Products

Pads: These are like the cozy sweaters of menstrual products—familiar and reliable. Sticking to the inside of your underwear, they catch blood after it exits your body. The pro side: they're super easy to use and great for beginners. The downside? They can feel bulky, and you need to change them every few hours to avoid leaks.

Tampons: Picture these as your on-the-go buddies. Inserted into the vagina, they soak up blood before it even bids farewell. They're fantastic for active days when you don't want anything slowing you down. The catch? There's a bit of a learning curve to using them, and it's crucial to change them regularly.

Menstrual Cups: These little champions are all about longevity and eco-friendliness. Made of medical-grade silicone, you fold and insert them, where they catch blood for up to 12 hours. The upside is fewer changes and less waste. On the flip side, they can take practice to insert comfortably, and cleaning requires a bit more effort.

Period Underwear: Imagine undies that do the job of a pad but feel like your favorite pair of cotton briefs. They're designed to absorb blood, offering a no-fuss approach to periods. Plus, they're reusable, making them kind to the planet. The downside? You need a few pairs to get through heavier days, and they can be an upfront investment.

Proper Use and Hygiene

Keeping things clean and changing products regularly is your golden ticket to having a happy period every month.

Here's the scoop on maintaining top-notch hygiene:

Pads and Tampons: Aim to change every four to six hours, even on light days. You can do this in order to keep things fresh and avoid any unwanted body odors or discomfort.

Menstrual Cups: These can hang out for up to 12 hours, but make sure you clean them thoroughly between uses with soap and water or according to the manufacturer's instructions.

Period Underwear: Treat these like your regular undies but with a superhero twist. Rinse them out after use and follow the care instructions for washing.

Disposal and Environmental Considerations

The planet thanks you for thinking about how you dispose of or reuse menstrual products:

Pads and Tampons: Always wrap these up and toss them in the trash. Flushing them can cause plumbing disasters (nobody wants that) and harm aquatic ecosystems. Looking for an eco-friendly option? Biodegradable pads and tampons say hello.

Period Cups and Underwear: These are the champions of reducing period waste. With proper care, period cups can last years, and the period undies can withstand countless washes, making them star players in the quest for a much easier period.

Period Hygiene Myths

Let's bust some myths that have been hanging around like uninvited guests at a party:

Myth: With the right products, like tampons or period cups, you can dive into the pool without a second thought.

Myth: Period blood is dirty. Fact: Period blood is just a mix of blood and tissue lining from your uterus. It's as natural as it gets, so let's ditch the stigma.

Myth: You shouldn't wash your hair on your period. Fact: This old wives' tale has no scientific backing. Wash your hair whenever you please!

Choosing the correct period products and practices is a personal journey, one that may take a lot of trial and error. Listen to your body, consider your lifestyle, and don't be afraid to try different options until you find your perfect match of products to use before, during and even after your period. Remember, your period is a natural part of life, and with the right tools and knowledge, you can tackle it with confidence and ease.

The Importance of a Healthy Diet During Puberty

Eating right during puberty is like choosing the best fuel for a rapidly growing and changing machine—your body. This period of life is like a construction zone where everything is expanding, shifting, and solidifying. It's not just about eating more; it's about eating smart. Let's break down the building blocks of a diet that supports you through these transformative years.

Nutrients Crucial for Puberty

Calcium: Think of calcium as the concrete that strengthens your bones. As you grow in height, your bones need all the support they can get. Dairy products like milk, cheese, and yogurt are packed with calcium. If dairy isn't your thing, leafy greens, almonds, and fortified plant milks are excellent alternatives for you to eat and drink.

Iron: This nutrient is like the workforce that keeps your energy levels up and it also supports healthy blood flow. Girls need more iron, especially once they start their period. Lean meats, spinach, beans, and fortified cereals can boost your iron intake.

Protein: Consider protein, the bricks laying down the foundation for muscle growth and repair. As your body grows, it leans heavily on protein. Chicken, tofu, legumes, and nuts are excellent sources.

Vitamins A, C, and E: These vitamins act like safety gear for your body. They protect your skin and eyes and support your immune system. Citrus fruits, carrots, sweet potatoes, and avocados are loaded with these vitamins.

Balancing Energy Intake

Your body during puberty is a bit like a car on a long road trip; it needs regular refueling. However, it's not about indiscriminately filling up the tank but ensuring the fuel is of good quality and the right amount. Listen to your hunger cues—they're your body's way of telling you it needs more energy for all the growing it's doing. Snack on nutrient-rich foods like fruits, nuts, and whole grains instead of reaching for sugary or highly processed options. Remember, your body is doing a lot of work; it deserves high-quality fuel every day.

Dealing with Cravings and Body Image

Cravings can hit like sudden thunderstorms, intense and out of the blue. It's okay to give in to them sometimes. After all, denying yourself your favorite treats can make you want them even more. The trick is all about having balance. Love chocolate? Pair a piece of chocolate with some fruit or nuts. Craving chips? Try them with a side of crunchy vegetables. It's all about not letting cravings pilot the plane.

During puberty, your body changes in ways that can feel strange, and it changes in strange ways, and it can be easy to be hard on yourself. Remember, these changes are your body's way of gearing up for adulthood. When you find yourself stressing over your image in the mirror, try to focus on what your body can do rather than just how it looks. It's an incredible vessel capable of amazing things—running, dancing, laughing. Feed it with kindness, both in thoughts and in nutrition. Believe in yourself that you are and will be able to make the right choices for your body, starting today.

Hydration

If nutrients are the building blocks, water is the mortar that holds everything together. Staying hydrated keeps your skin clear, your brain sharp, and your digestion smooth. If plain water sounds too bland, jazz it up with slices of lemon, cucumber, or berries. Keep a water bottle handy as a visual reminder to sip throughout the day. Drinking enough water also helps you distinguish between hunger and thirst, often confused signals during the rapid growth phase of puberty.

Eating well during puberty is not about strict diets or restrictions. Rather, it's about giving your body the fuel it needs in order for your body to do the incredible work it's doing every single day. By focusing on nutrient-rich foods, balancing your energy intake, treating yourself kindly, and staying hydrated, you're setting the stage for not just a healthy puberty but a healthy life, too.

Exercise and Your Body: Finding Fun in Movement

When puberty hits, it's like your body decides to throw a party and forgets to inform you. Suddenly, everything is changing, and it can feel a bit like navigating a maze in the dark. But here's a little secret: exercise is like turning on the lights. Not only does it help you see where you're going, but it also makes the journey a whole lot more fun. And the best part? The benefits stretch far beyond just the physical.

The Magic of Moving

First off, let's chat about why moving your body is like

sprinkling fairy dust over your puberty experience. Physically, it makes your muscles and bones grow while setting prime examples for those parts of your body. It also helps each part of your body prime your muscles and bones, setting a strong foundation for all of the growing that you're doing. solid . But the perks of your body working on itself don't stop there. Mentally, your body is hitting the play button on any form of exercise to release a playlist of feel-good hormones that can lift your mood faster than your favorite tune. Emotionally, your body and brain are it's a powerful allies. They are both teaching resilience and boosting confidence as you start noticing what your body is capable of.

Discovering Your Groove

Now, onto finding your exercise jam. The key? It's all about exploration and curiosity. The goal here isn't to become an Olympic athlete overnight (unless that's your dream, then, by all means, go for it!). It's about discovering what makes you feel alive, energized, and, most importantly, happy.

Team Sports: If you those who find joy in camaraderie, team sports might just be your thing. It's about more than just the game; it's the laughter, the shared victories, and even the losses that bond you with your teammates.

Solo Adventures: Maybe the thought of a quiet jog at dawn or a challenging hike speaks to your soul. Solo activities offer a unique kind of peace, allowing you to connect deeply with yourself.

Dance It Out: If music moves you, dance could be your perfect match. Whether it's ballet, hip-hop, or just freestyling in your room, dance is the celebration of movement that speaks every language.

Overcoming Hurdles

Let's face it, finding motivation can sometimes feel like searching for a needle in a haystack. And then there's the voice in your head whispering doubts and fears, especially when you're feeling self-conscious about your changing body.

Here's how to flip the script:

Schedule It: Treat your exercise time like any other necessary appointment. Putting it in your calendar makes it real and non-negotiable.

Small Steps: Rome wasn't built in a day, and your exercise habit won't be either. Start small and build up gradually. Celebrate every step forward, no matter how tiny.

Find Your Tribe: Sometimes, having a workout buddy can turn "I can't" into "I can." Together, you can encourage each other, share laughs, and make memories.

Keep it Fun: Remember, this is about finding joy in movement. Mix things up, create playlists, and turn your exercise time into the highlight of your day.

Celebrating Your Unique Journey

In a world plastered with images of "perfect" bodies, it's easy to fall into the comparison trap. Here's your gentle reminder that your body is on its own unique path, and that's something to celebrate, not criticize. Exercise isn't about achieving a specific look; it's about feeling strong, capable, and alive.

Focus on How You Feel: After you move, tune into how you feel. More often than not, you'll notice a surge of energy, a sense of accomplishment, and a brighter mood.

Set Personal Goals: Instead of aiming for a specific appearance, set goals related to your performance or how regularly you exercise. Maybe it's mastering a new yoga pose or adding an extra block to your run.

Be Kind to Yourself: Some days, you might not hit your goals, and that's okay. Your physical abilities Your physical abilities don't measure your worth. Show yourself the same kindness and encouragement you'd offer a friend.

In the grand adventure of puberty, exercise is much more than just a way to stay fit. It's a pathway to discovering your strengths, pushing your limits, and embracing the incredible capabilities of your changing body. So lace up those sneakers, take a deep breath, and step into the dance of movement with an open heart and an adventurous spirit. Who knows what unique places you'll find along the way?

Sleep and Puberty: Why Your Body Needs More Rest

In the whirlwind of changes that puberty brings, sleep becomes the unsung hero, working behind the scenes to support your journey. Think of sleep as your body's secret agent, aiding in everything from growth to brain development and even helping to keep your emotions in check. With all the physical and mental shifts happening, your body craves more restful nights to recharge and rejuvenate.

The Role of Sleep in Development

During sleep, your body isn't just resting; it's incredibly busy. Growth hormones do their heavy lifting while you're sleeping snoozing, contributing to the physical transformations of puberty. Your brain, meanwhile, is sorting through the day's experiences, solidifying memories, and even learning while you are asleep.

This nightly reset is crucial for emotional regulation, too, helping you navigate the rollercoaster of feelings puberty is known for.

Physical Growth: Those growth spurts need sleep to do their job well. It's when you're in the deepest stages of sleep that growth hormones are the most active.

Brain Development: Your brain uses sleep to process information, consolidate memories, and make sense of your emotions and social interactions.

Emotional Regulation: Adequate sleep helps balance your mood, reduces irritability and enhances your overall well-being.

Tips for Improving Sleep Quality

Creating a sleep sanctuary and a calming pre-bed routine can transform your nights from restless to restorative.

Here's how you can fine-tune your sleep environment and habits:

Reduce Screen Time: The blue light from screens can trick your brain into thinking it's daylight, hindering the production of sleep-inducing melatonin. Try winding down with a book or listening to calming music instead of screen time at least an hour before bed.

Create a Comfortable Sleep Space: Make your bedroom a haven for sleep. Keep it cool, dark, and quiet. Invest in a comfortable mattress and pillows that support a good night's rest.

Establish a Routine: Going to bed and waking up at the same time every day, even on weekends, can help regulate your body's internal clock and improve the quality of your sleep.

Dealing with Common Sleep Issues

Puberty can bring about sleep challenges that weren't on your radar before. If you find yourself tossing and turning, you're not alone.

Here are some strategies to tackle common sleep disturbances:

Difficulty Falling Asleep: Create a bedtime ritual that signals to your body and to your brain that it's time to wind down for the night. This could include reading, gentle stretching, or deep breathing exercises.

Sleep Disturbances: If you wake up in the middle of the night, keep the lights dim and engage in a quiet, calming activity until you feel sleepy again.

Restlessness: Regular physical activity during the day can help you get better sleep at night. Just do your best to avoid vigorous exercise close to bedtime, as it can have the opposite effect.

The Impact of Sleep Deprivation

Skimping on sleep can have more severe consequences than feeling groggy the next day. **Chronic sleep deprivation can affect every aspect of your life including but not limited to:**

Mood Swings: Lack of sleep can make you more susceptible to mood swings and emotional sensitivity, amplifying the already intense feelings puberty brings.

Academic Performance: Concentration, memory, and cognitive abilities suffer when one is not well-rested, making it harder to perform your best in school.

Physical Health: Ongoing sleep deprivation can weaken your immune system, making it easier for you to get sick. . Not getting enough sleep for a long period of time can even impact your long-term growth and development.

In essence, sleep is not a luxury; it's a non-negotiable, super-important pillar of protecting your health, especially during puberty. By prioritizing restful nights, you're not just investing in your physical growth and brain development; you're also giving yourself the emotional resilience and strength to navigate the changes and challenges puberty presents. So, tonight, as you prepare to drift off into dreamland, remember you're doing something powerful for yourself. You're laying the foundation for a healthy, balanced life.

The Truth About Body Odor: Tips and Tricks

When puberty rolls in, it's like flipping a switch on a whole host of changes, and body odor is one of those unanticipated guests that arrive at the party. It might seem like this new, more potent aroma is out to make life awkward, but it's actually a totally normal sign that your body is growing up.

Understanding Body Odor

So, why does body odor suddenly become a thing during puberty? It all boils down to sweat glands. Before puberty, sweat is pretty much odorless, but hormonal changes kick the apocrine glands into gear. The glands are found in areas like your underarms and groin, and they produce a thicker, more smelly kind of sweat. When this sweat mixes with the bacteria on your skin, voilà, you get that unwanted body odor. This doesn't mean you're doing anything wrong with your hygiene. It's just your body moving through another natural development phase of puberty.

Daily Hygiene Practices

Keeping body odor in check is mostly about sticking to a few daily habits. **Here's the breakdown:**

Wash daily: Taking a shower or bath every day with soap helps wash away sweat and the bacteria that love to feed on it.Pay extra attention to areas like your feet, underarms, and anywhere else you tend to sweat more.

Use deodorant: Applying deodorant to clean, dry underarms can help keep the smell of body odor away throughout the day. If you're sweating a lot, look for a product that's both an antiperspirant and deodorant. This type of product will help prevent the odor and feel of sweat on your body.

Wear clean clothes: Fresh clothes help you start the day off right. You can choose clothes that are made of natural fibers like cotton, which let your skin breathe.

Choosing Deodorants

Picking the right deodorant can feel like navigating another maze in this new phase of life called puberty.

Here's how to choose wisely:

Go for aluminum-free: If you have sensitive skin or if you are just cautious about the ingredients in your products, aluminum-free deodorants are a great option. They help mask odor without blocking your sweat pores.

Consider natural options: There are a growing number of natural deodorants out there. These deodorants are made from ingredients like baking soda, essential oils, and mineral salts. They can be gentler on young, sensitive skin and are worth a try if you're looking for a more eco-friendly option.

Test it out: Everyone's body chemistry is different. So what works for your friend might not work well for you. Don't be afraid to try out a few different types of deodorant until you find the one that works well with your body.

Dealing with Sweat

For some, sweating can feel like it's on overdrive during puberty

Here's what can help:

Dress smart: Try to wear loose-fitting clothes made of breathable fabrics. This can help keep air circulating and reduce sweat. Also, wearing light colors can help minimize the appearance of sweat marks on clothing, especially in the underarm region.

Stay cool: On hot days or when you're active, try taking breaks in cooler environments is a great idea to allow your body to cool down.

Mind your diet: Spicy foods and caffeine can actually make you sweat more. If sweating is a big concern, you might want to ease up on the caffeine and spicy foods, no matter how much you love them.

When to see a doctor: If your sweating is way more than what your friends experience or is seriously getting in the way of your day-to-day life, it could be a condition called hyperhidrosis. A talk with your doctor can offer solutions, which range from prescription antiperspirants to other treatments designed to keep excessive sweating under control.

Navigating the newness of body odor and sweating doesn't have to be stressful. You can feel more confident and comfortable in your skin with a few tweaks to your daily routine and the right products. You can feel more confident and comfortable in your skin with a few tweaks to your daily routine and the right products in your arsenal. Remember, everyone going through puberty is experiencing similar changes, so you're definitely not alone in this.

Dental Care: Keeping Your Smile Bright

Puberty is a bit like being handed the keys to a car without an instruction manual on how to work the car, much less being taught how actually to drive the car. Suddenly, you're in the driver's seat, navigating through a maze of changes, and yes, dental care becomes one of those unexpected turns in the road. Now, more than ever, your mouth is on the front lines, facing everything from battles with braces and the ever-dreaded cavities. Let's gear up, and polish your teeth). You can ensure your smile stays as radiant as your personality.

Importance of Dental Hygiene

You've probably heard it a million times: Brush your teeth.

But during puberty, this mantra takes on a whole new level of importance. Why? Because those dietary shifts—hello, midnight snacks and sudden sugar cravings—can leave your teeth more vulnerable to cavities. Plus, your mouth is part of the grand transformation your body is going through, meaning it's extra sensitive and needs all the TLC (Tender Loving Care) it can get.

Fight against cavities: Regular brushing and flossing keep those pesky cavities away, By brushing regularly, you're ensuring that your smile stays bright and pain-free.

Gum health: It's not just about the teeth; your gums need attention too. Healthy gums lay the foundation for a strong set of teeth.

Fresh breath: Let's not forget the confidence that comes from having fresh breath. It's like a secret weapon!

Effective Brushing and Flossing Techniques

Mastering the art of brushing and flossing is like learning a new dance routine; it's all about the moves.

Brushing: Aim for a two-minute routine, twice a day. Picture your mouth divided into four quadrants and spend 30 seconds on each. Use a soft-bristled brush to gently massage your teeth and gums in a circular motion, not forgetting the back molars and the tongue (a hotspot for bacteria).

Flossing: Flossing is the magic wand for those hard-to-reach spots between your teeth. Gently slide the floss up and down the sides of each tooth and under the gumline, using a clean section of floss for each tooth. Now, thanks to technology, there is a tool called the Waterpik that lets you floss your teeth with water. This tool allows you to find those hard-to-reach places you can't get to from regular flossing. It is more effective, and a faster way to floss, too.

In this chapter of your life, where every day feels like a new scene in the epic tale of puberty, dental care plays a critical role. It's not just about dodging and preventing cavities or mastering how to perfectly floss your teeth. It's about laying the groundwork for a lifetime of healthy smiles. So, embrace the journey, braces and all, knowing that each brush and each floss each floss is a step towards not just a brighter smile, but a healthier you.

Hair Care: Dealing with Oiliness and Dandruff

When puberty hits, your body decides to experiment with your hair's chemistry set, leading to changes that could rival any mad scientist's concoction. Suddenly, your hair might start acting like it's got a mind of its own—getting oilier by the minute or flaking like a winter snowstorm. Don't worry. It's all part of your body's grand plan, reacting to the hormonal shifts that puberty brings.

Changes in hair during puberty

Why does your hair start producing enough oil to rival a fast-food fryer or begin flaking like it's auditioning for a snow globe? Hormones, are the culprits here. They ramp up oil production in your hair , leading to that greasy feeling. On the flip side, those hormones can also cause your scalp to dry out and flake. It's your body's way of adjusting to the new hormonal landscape it finds itself in. While it can be annoying, it's completely normal.

Choosing the right hair care products

Navigating the hair care aisle at the store can feel like being a contestant on a game show where you have to pick the right door to win the grand prize—healthy hair. **Here's how to choose the correct hair products wisely:**

For oily hair: Look for shampoos that are labeled "volumizing," "strengthening," or "balancing." These are less moisturizing and won't weigh your hair down. Avoid products labeled "intensive moisturizing," as they can actually add to the oiliness.

For dry, flaky scalp: Moisturizing shampoos are your best friend. Ingredients like tea tree oil can help stop dandruff. If your scalp is sensitive, hypoallergenic shampoos are a safe bet. The words hypoallergenic shampoo mean that this type of shampoo is less likely than other brands of shampoo to cause you to have an allergic reaction.

Conditioners: A good conditioner can help keep your hair manageable regardless of scalp type. Apply it mainly to the ends of your hair to avoid greasy roots.

Washing frequency and techniques

How often you wash your hair can make a big difference. Washing too often can strip your hair of its natural oils, leading to more oil production. On the other hand, not washing enough can allow oil and flakes to build up.

Here's the balance:

Oily hair: If you have oily hair, you should wash it every other day.. This should keep the grease at bay without over-drying your scalp.

Dry, flaky scalp: If you have a dry, flaky scalp, you should you're your hair less frequently, about two to three times a week should do it. Staying consistent in that routine can help your scalp retain its natural moisture.

When washing, focus on putting the shampoo on your scalp where oil production is highest, and let the suds gently cleanse the rest of your hair as you rinse. Conditioner should be the opposite; When you use conditioner, you should concentrate on the ends of your hair to avoid greasy roots.

Natural remedies and when to seek help

Sometimes, the best solutions come from nature:

For oiliness: If your hair is oily, try rinsing it with diluted apple cider vinegar. It can help cut through the grease and balance your scalp's pH. Just a forewarning though, it doesn't smell pleasant.

For dandruff: If you still struggle with dandruff, try massaging Massaging your scalp with aloe vera gel before shampooing your scalp with aloe vera gel before shampooing. This can soothe and moisturize dry skin.

If you've tried managing oiliness or dandruff at home without success, or if your scalp is irritated, red, or excessively flaky, it might be time to talk with a dermatologist, also known as a skin doctor. They can provide targeted treatments that are specifically designed for you, like medicated shampoos or scalp treatments, to get your hair back on track.

Moving forward, remember that taking care of your hair is just one part of the bigger picture of taking care of yourself during puberty. Every step you take, whether it's choosing the right shampoo or learning to embrace the changes your body is going through, is a step toward becoming more in tune with yourself. As we shift our focus to the next chapter, keep in mind that self-care, in all its forms, is not just about looking good—it's about feeling good on the inside and embracing the journey of growing up with confidence and grace.

Chapter Three

Riding the Emotional Waves of Puberty

Imagine your emotions are like weather patterns, unique to your personal climate. Some days are sunny and bright, others might bring unexpected storms, and occasionally, you might find yourself in the midst of a whirlwind, wondering, "Where did this come from?" Puberty is a bit like climate change for your emotions; it intensifies feelings, mixes up patterns, and sometimes leaves you unprepared for the forecast. But just like any seasoned weather watcher, you can learn to predict, prepare for, and navigate through these emotional shifts with a toolkit at your side.

Understanding and Managing Your Emotions

Recognizing a Wide Range of Emotions

It's normal to experience a wide range of emotions during puberty. One minute, you're laughing; the next, you might feel like crying without any apparent reason. Think of your emotions as colors on a vast palette (just like a painter uses when they paint). Each with each one adding to the depth and complexity of the picture of who you are. It's okay not to feel okay sometimes, and it's equally okay to feel different emotions at the same time. Some of these emotions can include but aren't limited to feeling happy, excited, sad, angry, or anywhere in between. Acknowledging these feelings is the first step in understanding them.

Keeping an emotion journal: Jot down what you're feeling and when. Over time, you might start to see patterns, which can help you anticipate and manage your emotions better. There are so many fun and beautiful resources on how that you can use. Draw a grid with 31 blocks and assign a color to each mood (example, green = happy/okay). Color in a block each day of your general mood. You may begin to notice a pattern!

Emotion charades with friends: Sometimes, sharing and guessing emotions with friends in a fun setting can make you feel less alone in your experiences.

Healthy Expression of Feelings

Finding healthy ways to express your emotions can turn potentially overwhelming situation into a manageable one. Whether it's talking to someone you trust about how you're feeling, channeling your emotions into creative outlets like art or music, or releasing energy through physical activity, there are many ways to navigate through your feelings.

Create a playlist: Music can mirror your emotions, and creating playlists for different moods can be both therapeutic and a way to express how you're feeling without words.

Start a creative project: Whether it's painting, writing, or dancing, working on a project can help channel your emotions into something tangible.

The Impact of Hormones on Emotions

Hormonal changes during puberty can intensify your emotions making you feel more intense joy, sadness, anger, or frustration. Understand that these fluctuations in your emotions are a normal part of growing up. Realizing this can help you take a step back and recognize that these intense feelings will pass.

Educate yourself: Learning about the hormonal changes happening in your body can demystify why you're feeling a certain way and remind you that it's a temporary state.

Coping Mechanisms for Tough Days

We all have those days when emotions feel too heavy to carry. Having a set of coping mechanisms can act like a life raft, keeping you afloat until the waters calm down.

Mindfulness and breathing exercises: Techniques like deep breathing, meditation, or yoga can center your thoughts and calm your mind. A good walk in nature can be life-changing!

Seeking support: Sometimes, talking to a friend, family member, or counselor can provide comfort and perspective. Knowing when to ask for help is a sign of strength and self-awareness. It is never a sign of weakness.

Using humor: Finding something to laugh about, even on tough days, can lighten your mood and offer a break from the intense emotions that you're feeling.

Creativity: Sometimes, just getting it out makes the world of a difference! On really tough days, it is up to you to find what will make you feel better—whether it's writing your thoughts down or scribbling with some colorful pens! And a go-to favorite for a lot of people your age, is some uplifting and happy music.

Puberty is a time of significant change, and navigating through the emotional ups and downs requires patience, understanding, and a bit of preparation. Remember, every emotion, like every weather pattern, is temporary. With the right strategies, you can learn to confidently ride the waves of your feelings, knowing that sunny days are always on the horizon.

The Impact of Puberty on Your Self-Esteem

Puberty tosses you into a sea of physical transformations, each wave bringing a change that might make you glance in the mirror a bit longer, pondering, "Is this really me?" It's like your body decided to hit the fast-forward button, leaving your self-image scrambling to catch up. This whirlwind of change can mess up your self-esteem, making it wobble. When you hit puberty, you might often be faced with doubts about your appearance, abilities, friends, and family. You also might ask yourself whether you're good enough in school or sports, a good enough friend, or a good enough daughter to your parents.

The Dance Between Physical Changes and Self-Esteem

When your reflection starts to shift, it's as if you're meeting someone new for the first time—except that someone is you. Suddenly, your clothes fit differently, your voice might change its tune, and acne could decide to make a grand entrance. Each of these changes is like a note in the complex melody and song of puberty, and it's natural if some notes feel off-key, straining your relationship with your self-image. There are steps you can take to lessen the hit your self-image and self-esteem takes during puberty.

Acknowledge the change: Recognizing that your body is supposed to change during this time is like finding your footing on shaky ground. It's the first step in moving towards accepting your ever-evolving self.

Separate feelings from facts: Your feelings about your changing body are valid, but they don't define your worth or dictate the whole story of who you are. It is also so important to remember that feelings are not permanent and will change. sometimes, your feelings will change rapidly.

Crafting a Positive Body Image

Building a fortress of positive body image in the midst of puberty's onslaught requires a lot of self-acceptance, as well as an appreciation for what your body can do, and the confidence to reinforcement of challenging societal beauty standards.

Highlight body functionality: Celebrate your body for what it can do—run, dance, breathe, laugh—rather than just how it appears. This appreciation for functionality over appearance is a cornerstone of positive body image.

Question beauty standards: Society's blueprint of beauty is more like a rough sketch than a detailed plan. Questioning why certain body types are celebrated over others can dismantle the power these standards hold over you.

The Mirror of Media and Social Comparison

In today's digital age, social media acts as a mirror, reflecting images that can either distort or clarify our perception of beauty. This mirror often magnifies your insecurities, making it easy to tumble down the rabbit hole of comparison.

Curate your feed: Fill your social media with accounts that uplift and reflect the diversity of human beauty. It's like choosing the music that plays in your life—make sure it lifts your spirits.

Reality check: Remember, what glitters on screen might not be gold. Many images are airbrushed to an unrealistic perfection, a far cry from the unfiltered beauty that is really behind every girl's smile. Remember, you never need makeup to be beautiful.

Celebrating Individuality

Embracing your unique qualities is like planting a flag on the peak of a mountain, declaring and celebrating, "This is me." Your individual traits—those freckles, your unruly hair, the way you snort when you laugh—are the chapters of your story that make your journey through this thing called life unlike anyone else's.

Spotlight on strengths: Shift the focus to your strengths, skills, and talents. Maybe you're a wizard with words, a sports prodigy, or a kindness ninja. These attributes are the real gems that sparkle, regardless of the puberty changes that you're navigating.

Create a self-love jar: Fill a jar with notes of things you like about yourself—traits, achievements, compliments you've received. When self-doubt creeps in, pull out a note as a reminder of your worth.

Navigating the emotional landscape of puberty, with its peaks and valleys, requires a map of self-awareness, a compass of self-compassion, and the willingness to trek through unfamiliar territories. It's a voyage where you learn to chart your own course, discovering along the way that true beauty and worth are found in the uniqueness of your journey and the courage with which you travel it.

Body Positivity: Embracing Your Body's Changes

Body positivity is your cheer squad in the arena of self-acceptance. It's the voice that champions your right to feel fabulous in your skin, no matter the size, shape, or any of those quirky bits that make you, well, you. Body positivity is about loving and respecting your body as it navigates the puberty and growing up. It's about high-fiving yourself in the mirror because, hey, you're pretty awesome! Why does it matter, you ask? Picture this: you're building a skyscraper (that's you, growing up!). Body positivity is the steel frame that keeps the building standing tall, no matter how strong the winds of change blow. It's the foundation that lets you face the world with confidence, knowing you're more than just a reflection in the mirror. It's vital because it shapes not just how you see yourself, but how you interact with the world around you.

Challenging Beauty Norms

Now, onto shaking up those beauty norms. Society has the cookie-cutter image of beauty, but guess what? Real life isn't a cookie-cutter affair at all. **Here's how you can toss those societal standards out the window:**

Spotlight on diversity: Celebrate the vast spectrum of human beauty. From freckles to curves, from tall to petite, beauty comes in an endless array. Highlighting and valuing diversity challenges the narrow definitions that often crowd media portrayals.

Model rebellion: Be the change. Wear what makes you happy, style your hair (or don't) in ways that make you feel good, and let your unique light shine. When you confidently embrace your look, you're silently encouraging others to do the same.

Dialogue and discussion: Discuss body image and beauty standards with friends and family. Discussing how unrealistic expectations affect us can open eyes and minds to a broader, more inclusive view of beauty.

Affirmations and Self-Love Practices

Words have power, and affirmations are your magic spells for summoning self-love. **Here are a few affirmations to whisper, shout, or sing in front of the mirror every day:**

"I am strong, capable, and smart. My body is just one part of my incredible journey."

"Every day, in every way, I am learning to love myself a little more."

"I celebrate my body for all the amazing things it allows me to experience."

Pair these affirmations with practices that nurture self-love:

Gratitude journaling: Each night, jot down three things about your body you're grateful for. It could be as simple as "My legs that let me dance," or "My eyes that see beauty everywhere."

Mindful self-care: Make self-care a ritual. Whether it's a skincare routine, a relaxing bath, or a few minutes of stretching, do it with full attention and appreciation for your body.

Dealing with Negative Body Talk

If there's one thing that can rain on your body positivity parade, it's negative body talk. This can come from others or, often, from ourselves. **Here's how to stop the negative body talk:**

Flip the script: When you catch yourself or someone else dishing out negative talk about bodies, challenge it. Replace it with a positive or neutral statement. For example, "I hate my thighs" can become "My thighs are strong and carry me through my day."

Boundary setting: It's okay to tell friends or family that body shaming or negative talk isn't welcome in your space. Setting these boundaries protects not just your mental space, but it also fosters a healthier environment for everyone involved.

Compassion and understanding: Negative body talk often stems from someone else's insecurities or struggles. Approach these situations with empathy, offering support and encouraging a kinder perspective towards yourself and others.

By weaving body positivity into your daily life, you're not just building a healthier relationship with yourself; you're also contributing to making a better, more positive world where everyone can feel valued and beautiful in their own special and unique way. Remember, your body is the only one you've got—it's your home, your temple, and your best friend, all rolled into one. Treating it with love, respect, and kindness isn't just an act of self-care; it's a revolution.

Dealing with Comparison and Social Media Pressure

In the whirlwind of emotions and changes that come with growing up , social media can sometimes feel like a spotlight shining directly on all your insecurities. It's easy to fall into the trap of comparing your behind-the-scenes with everyone else's highlight reel. But here's the thing: your value isn't determined by likes, comments, or the images you see online.

Let's unpack how to steer through the social media landscape without letting it steer you.

Navigating Social Media Wisely

When not handled with care, social media can be a slippery slope leading straight to the awful comparison trap. It's a space where reality often takes a backseat to perfection. leaves you feeling as though you're not measuring up. But it doesn't have to be that way.

With a few mindful strategies, you can enjoy social media without letting it hurt your self-esteem:

Limit scrolling time: Spending too much time on social media can blur the lines between reality and fantasy. By setting specific times for checking apps such as Facebook, Instagram and Twitter, you give yourself the chance to engage with the real world more fully, appreciating your life and the people in it.

Follow accounts that inspire: Fill your feed with positivity. Follow accounts that inspire you, make you laugh, and remind you of the beauty in being perfectly imperfect. Unfollow or hide accounts that trigger negative feelings or comparisons.

Engage actively, not passively: Instead of mindlessly scrolling, engage actively. Leave kind comments, share content that resonates with you, and use social media to connect rather than compare.

Reality vs. Online Personas

The gap between online personas and reality can be bigger than you ever expected. It's important to remind yourself that what you see online is often a created version of someone's life, and those images of someone's life are selectively cropped and filtered.

Here's how to keep this perspective:

Remind yourself of the editing: Behind every "perfect" photo is a camera roll of outtakes. Remember, what's shared online is often the best of the best, selectively chosen from many not-so-perfect moments.

Talk about the discrepancies: Have open conversations with friends about the difference between social media and real life. Sharing your experiences can help clear up the perceived perfection and remind you that everyone has challenges, no matter what their profile might suggest.

Strategies to Reduce Comparison

Comparison can sneak up on you, especially when everyone's milestones and best moments are just a click away. However, reducing comparison and focusing on your own path is achievable:

Celebrate your achievements: Make a habit of celebrating your own milestones, no matter how small they may be. Whether it's a personal best in a run, mastering a new recipe, or simply getting through a tough day, you deserve to celebrate yourself at certain times. Acknowledging your achievements helps shift the focus back to you and your journey.

Practice gratitude: Start or end your day by listing three things you're grateful for. Shift your focus to what you have rather than what you think you lack can significantly reduce feelings of envy and of not being good enough.

Embrace your uniqueness: Remember, no one else has your combination of talents, experiences, and perspectives. Celebrate the things that make you uniquely you, rather than wishing for someone else's strengths.

Setting Healthy Boundaries with Technology

In an age where we're almost always plugged in, setting boundaries with technology is critical for mental and emotional well-being.

Designate tech-free times: Whether it's during meals, an hour before bed, or Sunday mornings, having tech-free times can help you disconnect from the digital world and reconnect with yourself and those around you.

Curate a positive feed: Take control of your digital environment by taking control of your social media feed. Follow accounts that make you feel good about yourself, and don't hesitate to mute or unfollow those that don't.

Be mindful of your online time: Track your time online and your activities. If social media is taking up more time than you'd like, consider using apps that limit your usage or set reminders on your phone, tablet or computer to take breaks.

Social media and the pressure to compare are just parts of the landscape of growing up in a digital age. By navigating these waters with intention and care, you can protect your self-esteem and develop a healthier relationship with your online world. Remember, the only fair comparison is the one between who you are now and who you aim to be—everyone else's journey is their own.

Building Confidence: Tips and Exercises

Navigating puberty isn't just about coping with the physical and emotional changes; it's also a prime time to create a garden of self-confidence. This isn't about creating an ego for yourself. Instead, it's about nurturing a sense of self-worth that allows you to stand tall, even when the winds of doubt and comparison try to break you. Here's how to water and grow that garden, ensuring it's lush and vibrant, ready to support you through puberty and throughout your life.

Identifying Your Strengths

Finding your strengths is like uncovering hidden treasures within yourself. Sometimes these gems are buried deep, requiring a bit of digging, but once discovered, they shine brightly, illuminating your path and empowering your journey. **Here's how to start your treasure hunt:**

Reflect on compliments: Think about the compliments you've received. What others admire in us can often help us figure out our strengths.

Explore different activities: Sometimes, our strengths surprise us, emerging from new experiences or challenges. the arts, you can discover talents you didn't know you had.

Create a 'win' wall: Dedicate a space in your room where you can display anything that makes you proud—artwork, awards, or even a list of personal achievements. Seeing your accomplishments daily in your room boosts your self-esteem and reminds you of your strengths.

Goal Setting and Personal Growth

Setting goals is like drawing a map for your treasure hunt; it guides your steps and keeps you focused on the prize. Goals related to personal growth and resilience are especially valuable during puberty, as they help you navigate this time with purpose and direction.

Here's how to set goals and obtain personal growth:

Start small: Big achievements start with small steps. Setting achievable goals builds momentum and confidence.

Make it measurable: Whether it's improving a grade in a subject you're struggling with, learning a new skill, or making time for self-care, having a clear, measurable goal allows you to see your progress.

Celebrate milestones: Every step towards your goal deserves recognition. Celebrating milestones, no matter how small, reinforces your commitment to achieving your goals and boosts your self-esteem.

Confidence-Building Exercises

Stepping outside your comfort zone is where growth happens. It's the training ground for confidence, teaching yourself that you're capable of more than you might think.

Here are a few exercises to stretch those confidence muscles:

Public speaking: Whether it's a class presentation or speaking up in a group, public speaking is a powerful way to boost your confidence. Start by speaking in smaller, more comfortable settings and gradually increase your audience size.

Try new activities: Joining a club, learning a new instrument, or picking up a sport—new activities challenge you to adapt and learn, building confidence along the way.

Volunteering: Offering your time and skills to help others not only contributes to your community but also builds self-esteem. It reminds you of your abilities and the positive impact you can have.

The Power of Positive Peer Influence

The company you keep can act like sunlight and water to your garden of confidence, nurturing its growth or casting shadows that hinder it. Surrounding yourself with positive influences is critical during puberty, a time when you're more susceptible to people's outside opinions.

Here's how to cultivate a supportive social circle:

Choose friends who uplift you: Seek out friends who celebrate your successes, offer kind words, and encourage you to pursue your goals. These are the people who bring out the best in you.

Be that friend: Confidence grows in a culture of support. Be the friend who uplifts others, offering encouragement and celebrating their achievements. It's a cycle of positivity that boosts everyone's confidence.

Distance from negativity: If there are individuals in your life who consistently bring you down or dampen your spirit, it might be time to reconsider those relationships. Protecting your confidence sometimes means setting boundaries with those who challenge it without cause.

Building confidence during puberty is about embracing

your journey, recognizing your strengths, and surrounding yourself with positivity. It's about setting goals that stretch you and finding joy in the challenge. With each step outside your comfort zone and every achievement, big or small, your confidence will grow and , create a environment that supports you through puberty and throughout your life.

The Power of Positive Self-Talk

Imagine your thoughts as tiny seeds. Some can grow into lush, vibrant flowers, while others might sprout into prickly weeds if you're not careful about which ones you water. This is the essence of self-talk—the ongoing dialogue you can have with yourself that can uplift or undermine, depending on its nature. Understanding and nurturing positive self-talk is like choosing to cultivate a garden of flowers; it's about fostering growth, beauty, and strength within yourself.

Understanding Self-Talk

Every thought that goes through your mind, from "I can do this" to "I'm not good enough," is a form of self-talk. These internal whispers are powerful. They can shape how you view yourself, influence your emotions, and guide your behaviors. There's a big contrast between positive and negative self-talk. Positive self-talk is like a supportive friend, encouraging and optimistic, while negative self-talk is the critic that finds your faults and only increases the doubts that you may have about yourself.

Recognizing the difference is step one in transforming how you converse with yourself.

Spotting negative patterns: Pay attention to moments when you're being particularly hard on yourself. Are there common themes or situations that trigger this?

Reframing exercises: Practice flipping negative statements on their head. For instance, change "I always mess up" to "I learn from my mistakes."

Transforming Negative Self-Talk

Transitioning from a harsh inner critic to a nurturing inner voice doesn't happen overnight. It's a process, one that involves mindfulness and a dash of creativity.

Affirmation creation: Craft your own personal affirmations that resonate with you. These positive statements can counterbalance negative thoughts. For example, "I am capable of achieving my goals" can be a powerful antidote to doubt.

Visualization: Picture yourself succeeding or handling a situation with ease. Visualization can increase your self-esteem and transform your internal dialogue.

Letter to yourself: Write a letter from the perspective of your best friend. What would they say about you? This exercise can help shift your perspective and highlight your positive attributes.

The Role of Mindfulness in Self-Talk

Mindfulness is about being present and fully engaged with the now. It's being fully aware of your thoughts, feelings, and surroundings without judgment. Applying mindfulness to self-talk means observing your thoughts without getting tangled in them.

Mindful breathing: When you catch your thoughts spiraling, pause for a mindful breathing exercise. Counting your breaths can help center your thoughts and give you space to choose a kinder response to yourself.

Thought observation: Try to observe your thoughts as if they were leaves floating down a stream. Notice them, but let them pass without attaching to them.

This practice can help you identify negative self-talk without letting it define how you truly feel about yourself.

Practicing Gratitude

Gratitude is a powerful tool for shifting focus from what's lacking to what's abundant in your life. It's about appreciating the big and small, from the roof over your head to the warmth of a friend's smile. Embedding gratitude into your daily routine can alter your mental landscape, watering those seeds of positive thoughts until they bloom.

Gratitude journal: Dedicate a few minutes each evening to writing down three things you're grateful for. Over time, this practice can shift your inner dialogue toward the positive.

Gratitude reminders: Set random alarms throughout your day as reminders to pause and reflect on something you're grateful for. It could be as simple as the sun on your face or a message from a friend.

Incorporating these practices into your life doesn't just alter your self-talk; it transforms it into a wellspring of positivity, nourishing your self-esteem and emotional well-being. Remember, the dialogue you have with yourself sets the tone for your life's story. Make it one filled with kindness, encouragement, and gratitude, and watch as your world transforms, one positive thought at a time.

Navigating Friendships: Changes and Challenges

Growing up, we often think of friendships as these unchanging bonds that will always stay the same throughout our lives, like our favorite pair of sneakers that never seem to wear out. But then puberty hits, and suddenly, it feels like everything, including friendships, is in flux. It's as if you've been sailing smoothly on calm waters, and out of nowhere, you find yourself navigating through choppy seas. This is all part of growing up; honestly, it's how you can find your true crew, the kind of friends that stick with you through thick and thin.

Evolving Friendships During Puberty

When puberty rolls around, it's like someone turned up the dial on life. Everything feels more intense, including our friendships. You might start to notice that the interests you shared with your best friend in grade school aren't aligning anymore. Maybe you're into sports now, and they've got their head buried in science fiction novels. It's not that anyone did anything wrong; it's just that as we grow, our paths sometimes diverge, leading us to new interests and different social circles.

Embrace the change: Recognize that changing interests is a normal part of growing up. It doesn't mean you have to lose old friends, but it might mean your relationship evolves in new ways.

Explore new social circles: Join clubs or teams that align with your newfound interests. It's a great way to meet people who share your passions.

Making and Maintaining Healthy Friendships

Finding and keeping friends during this whirlwind period of life requires a bit of effort, but it's worth it. Healthy friendships are those that make you feel good about yourself, where there's mutual respect, shared interests, and boundaries that everyone respects.

Be yourself: The best friendships are those where you can be your true self. Pretending to be someone you're not is like wearing a mask – it gets uncomfortable after a while.

Communication is key: Open and honest communication helps strengthen bonds. If something bothers you, find a gentle way to bring it up. Chances are, your friend might not even realize there is an issue.

Dealing with Conflicts and Jealousy

Even the strongest friendships can hit rough waters, especially when jealousy or misunderstandings come into play. Maybe you're feeling left out because your friend made the soccer team and you didn't, or there's a new person in your friend group, and the dynamics are shifting.

Talk it out: If you're feeling jealous or hurt, talk to your friend about it. Often, these feelings come from your insecurities, and just voicing them can help lighten the load that you may be feeling.

Focus on solutions: Instead of dwelling on the problem, try to think of ways to improve the situation. Maybe it's finding a new activity both you and your friend enjoy or setting aside more one-on-one time to hang out with each other.

The Importance of Supportive Friendships

In the tapestry of life, friends are the colorful threads that add richness and texture. They cheer us on, pick us up when we're down, and make the mundane moments memorable. Having friends who support you, understand you, and make you feel valued is like finding treasure—it's priceless.

Seek positivity: Surround yourself with people who lift you up and encourage you to be the best version of yourself. Life's too short to spend it with those who bring you down.

Be that friend: Remember, friendship is a two-way street. Be the supportive, kind, and understanding friend you wish to have. It's in giving that we receive, and often, the love and support we put out into the world find their way back to us.

As you sail through the turbulent waters of puberty, remember that friendships are evolving just like you. Embrace the changes, communicate openly, and cherish those who make this journey a little brighter. After all, it's the friends we choose to bring along on our adventure that make all the difference.

experiences crushes and it's okay to have them. They're a sign that your emotions are expanding, giving you a glimpse into the world of romantic feelings.

Crushes and How to Handle New Feelings

Stepping into the world of crushes and fluttery feelings is like opening a door to a room you never knew existed in your house. Suddenly, there's a whole new space in your head and in your heart filled with emotions you've never felt so strongly before. It's thrilling, confusing, and sometimes a bit scary. But hey, it's all part of growing up. Let's navigate this new territory together, shall we?

Understanding New Romantic Feelings

When puberty hits, it's like your heart gets upgraded to a more sensitive version. Suddenly, you might find yourself noticing people in a way you haven't before. Crushes are those warm, fuzzy feelings you get when you think about someone you like. It's all thanks to our hormones; they're the ones throwing the party and inviting all these new emotions into your daily life. Remember, developing a crush on someone is entirely normal and a natural part of discovering who you are and what you like in other people.

Normalizing the experience: First, understand that everyone experiences crushes, and it's okay to have them. They're a sign that your emotions are expanding, giving you a glimpse into the world of romantic feelings.

Managing Emotions Associated with Crushes

Having a crush can feel like riding an emotional roller coaster. One minute, you're up in the clouds, and the next, you might be down in the dumps, especially if you're unsure if your crush likes you too. Managing these emotions requires a mix of self-awareness and strategies to keep your feelings in check.

Keep a journal: Writing down your thoughts and feelings can help you process what you're going through. It's a safe space to express yourself and reflect on your emotions.

Stay grounded: Remind yourself that it's okay to have a crush on someone, but it shouldn't take over your life. Keep engaging in the activities you love, spending time with friends, and focusing on school.

Healthy Expressions of Affection

Expressing your feelings to someone you have a crush on is a big step, and it's important to do it in a respectful and considerate way. Remember, your feelings are valid, but so are theirs, and they might not feel the same way.

Here's how to express your affection healthily:

Start with friendship: Getting to know your crush as a friend first can lay a good foundation. It allows you to build a connection based on mutual interests and respect.

Be honest and direct: If you decide to express your feelings, be honest but gentle. A simple "I really enjoy spending time with you and was wondering if you'd like to go out sometime?" can open the door to the next step without putting too much pressure on either of you.

Respect their response: Whether they share your feelings or not, respect their response. Remember, someone not returning your feelings doesn't diminish your worth or desirability.

Dealing with Rejection Gracefully

Not every crush will turn into a love story, and that's perfectly okay. Rejection is a part of life and handling it with grace is a skill worth developing.

Here's how to navigate those moments:

Allow yourself to feel: It's okay to be sad or disappointed. Allow yourself to feel those emotions, but don't let them define you.

Talk to someone you trust: Sharing how you're feeling with a friend, family member, or even a journal can help you process your emotions.

Focus on self-love: Remind yourself of your strengths and qualities. Rejection doesn't reflect your worth; it's simply an indication that this particular match wasn't right.

Keep moving forward: Engage in activities that make you happy and help you grow. This can be a time for self-discovery and developing new interests.

Navigating the world of crushes and new romantic feelings is like adding a new dimension to your emotional landscape. It's exciting, sometimes nerve-wracking, but always a learning experience. By understanding these feelings, managing your emotions, expressing affection healthily, and dealing with rejection gracefully, you're not just surviving your crushes; you're learning valuable lessons about love, respect, and self-worth. And remember, each experience, whether it ends in heartache or in a heart-flutter, is shaping you into a more empathetic, resilient, and loving person. So, take a deep breath, muster your courage, and let your heart lead the way. Who knows where it might take you?

Setting Boundaries: Learning to Say No

Navigating the busy streets of puberty, where every corner seems to present a new challenge or experience, learning to set boundaries is like having your own personal road map. It's the skill that helps you decide which paths are right for you and which ones you'd rather not travel. Boundaries are your invisible lines that mark where your comfort zone ends and where the outside world begins. They help protect your emotional and physical well-being, making sure you stay true to yourself among the whirlwind of changes that take place.

The Importance of Boundaries

Setting personal boundaries is crucial, not just for your peace of mind, but for your overall health. It's about knowing and communicating your limits, what you're okay with, and what makes you feel uncomfortable or stressed. Having clear boundaries is like wearing an invisible suit of armor; it shields you from situations that can drain your energy or lead to unnecessary stress. Whether it's saying no to a late-night hangout because you need sleep, or not wanting to share personal details with someone you don't trust, boundaries help you navigate puberty with confidence and ease.

Visualize your boundaries: Picture yourself in a situation that makes you uncomfortable. What line would you not want others to cross? Asking yourself this question can help you start identifying your boundaries.

Reflect on your values: Your boundaries often come from your core values. Understanding what matters most to you can guide you in setting limits that reflect these priorities.

Identifying and Communicating Boundaries

Knowing your boundaries is one thing, but communicating them clearly to others is where the real challenge lies. It's like having a map but also needing the right words to describe the route. When it comes to sharing your boundaries with friends, family, or romantic interests, clarity and kindness go hand in hand. It's not about building walls between you and others; it's about laying down clear markers that help relationships grow healthily and respectfully.

Practice 'I' statements: Frame your boundaries in terms of your feelings and needs. For example, "I feel overwhelmed when I don't have time to myself. I need to spend some evenings alone to recharge."

Be direct but compassionate: Honesty doesn't have to be harsh. You can be firm about your limits while still showing care for the other person's feelings.

Respecting Others' Boundaries

Just as you cherish your own boundaries, it's vital to extend the same respect to others. Recognizing and honoring the limits set by friends and family is a cornerstone of healthy relationships. It's a two-way street; by showing that you value their comfort and limits, you foster an environment where mutual respect thrives. When someone communicates their boundaries to you, listen actively, acknowledge their needs, and adjust your behavior accordingly. It's like a dance where both partners are in tune, ensuring no one's toes get stepped on.

Ask questions: If you're unsure about someone's boundaries, just ask. It shows you care about their comfort and are willing to make adjustments.

Apologize if you overstep: We all make mistakes. If you accidentally cross someone's boundary, a sincere apology can go a long way in mending fences.

Dealing with Boundary Violations

Despite your best efforts, there might be times when your boundaries are disregarded and in other words, violated. It can feel like a storm cloud looming over your newly cultivated garden of self-respect. The key here is not to retreat but to stand firm, reinforcing your boundaries with confidence. Seek support from trusted friends or adults if you're dealing with persistent violations, especially if they impact your emotional or physical well-being. Remember, you have the right to feel safe and respected in all your relationships.

Stay firm: Reiterate your boundary clearly and calmly. Sometimes, people need to hear it more than once to fully grasp its importance.

Seek support: If someone continuously disrespects your boundaries, don't hesitate to reach out for help. Whether it's a counselor, teacher, or family member, having an ally can strengthen your resolve.

In the end, setting and respecting boundaries is about creating a life where you feel respected, safe, and empowered. It's a skill that will serve you well beyond puberty, helping you navigate the complexities of relationships throughout your life. As we wrap up this chapter, remember that your feelings and comfort matter. Setting boundaries is not just an act of self-care; it's a declaration of and to your worth. As you continue on your journey, let this understanding guide you in building connections that are healthy, respectful, and enriching. Now, with our boundaries firmly in place, let's move forward, ready to explore new territories with confidence and a strong sense of self.

Chapter Four

connecting with others

Picture this: you've got a giant puzzle in front of you, but instead of a picture on the box, you're left to figure out how the pieces fit together on your own. That's a lot like navigating the ups and downs of puberty, especially when it comes to talking about your feelings and making sure you're heard and understood. So, let's grab those puzzle pieces and start fitting them together, one conversation at a time.

Communication Skills: Talking About Your Feelings

The Power of Effective Communication

Think of communication as the glue that holds relationships together. It's what turns misunderstandings into mutual understanding and strengthens the bonds between you and the people around you. But here's the catch: not all communication is created equal. Clear, honest conversations about how you're feeling can sometimes feel as challenging as hitting a high note in your favorite song. Yet, mastering this skill is like unlocking a superpower that can transform your relationships.

Why it matters: Imagine you're in a group project, and someone keeps overriding your ideas. If you keep quiet, frustration simmers. But if you speak up, explaining how you feel overlooked, it opens the door to a solution. That's effective communication in action.

Expressing Emotions Appropriately

Ever noticed how a simple "I'm fine" can actually mean a whole lot more? It's like when you're texting and use a period instead of an exclamation point – suddenly, everything feels more serious. **Here's how to express what you're truly feeling without the guesswork:**

Use 'I' statements: Instead of saying, "You never listen to me," try "I feel unheard when my ideas aren't considered." It's less about blaming and more about expressing your perspective.

Active listening: It's a two-way street. When you're sharing your feelings, genuinely listen to responses without planning your next argument. It's like catching a ball – you have to be ready to receive it.

Overcoming Communication Barriers

Sometimes, it feels like there's an invisible wall between you and the person you're trying to talk to. Maybe it's fear of being judged or worrying they won't understand.

Here's how to break down those walls:

Identify the barriers: Recognize what's holding you back. Is it fear of their reaction or not knowing the right words? Pinpointing the issue is the first step to overcoming it.

Small steps: Start with less intimidating conversations and work your way up. It's like warming up before a big game – you've got to stretch those communication muscles.

Practicing Empathy

Empathy is all about putting yourself in someone else's shoes. It's imagining how they feel based on their perspective, not just your own. In conversations, this is like adding color to a black-and-white picture – it brings depth and understanding.

Ask questions: Show genuine interest in their feelings and experiences. Questions like "How did that make you feel?" or "What would you like me to understand about this situation?" can open up new levels of conversation.

Reflect back: After listening, summarize what you've heard in your own words. It shows you're truly engaged and helps clarify any misunderstandings right away.

Communication isn't just about talking; it's about connecting with someone on a level that goes beyond words. It's the bridge that allows you to cross over to someone else's experience, understanding their feelings, and sharing your own. Like any skill, it takes practice, patience, and a good dose of courage. But once you get the hang of it, you'll find that expressing your emotions and understanding others becomes less of a puzzle and more of a shared journey.

How to Talk to Adults About Puberty

Navigating conversations about puberty with adults can sometimes feel like trying to solve a Rubik's Cube—complex, frustrating, but ultimately rewarding when you get it right. It's a dance of timing, preparation, and understanding diverse perspectives, all while standing firm in your own experience. Here's how to approach these talks with confidence and clarity.

Choosing the Right Moment

Timing is everything, especially when you're about to dive into topics as personal as puberty. It's like waiting for the perfect wave to surf; you need patience and observation to know when to go for it.

Look for calm waters: Choose a time when both you and the adult are relaxed and not rushed. This could be during a quiet car ride, after dinner, or on a weekend morning.

Private spaces are key: : Find a spot where you won't be interrupted or overheard. This could be at home, during a walk, or anywhere else you feel comfortable and at ease.

Preparing for the Conversation

Going into these conversations without a plan is like setting sail without a map. Here's how to chart your course:

List your topics: Write down what you want to discuss. This could range from questions about physical changes to how you're feeling emotionally. Seeing your thoughts on paper can help you organize them better.

Practice makes perfect: Try rehearsing what you want to say out loud, maybe in front of a mirror or with a trusted friend. This can help you feel more confident in expressing yourself clearly.

Finding Support if Needed

Sometimes, despite your best efforts, conversations don't go as planned. Maybe the adult doesn't understand, or perhaps you couldn't quite express yourself the way you wanted. It's like when a recipe doesn't turn out right—you need a backup plan.

Have a plan B: Identify another adult you trust and feel comfortable talking to. This could be another family member, a teacher, or a school counselor.

Professional help: If your concerns are more serious or you're not getting the support you need at home, consider reaching out to a healthcare provider or therapist who specializes in adolescent health.

Appreciating Diverse Perspectives

Remember, adults come with their own set of experiences and cultural backgrounds, which can influence how they view and talk about puberty. It's like trying on different pairs of glasses, each pair offers a unique view of the world.

Be open to different views: Try to understand where they're coming from, even if it differs from your perspective. This can open up a more meaningful dialogue.

Agree to disagree: It's okay to have different opinions. What's important is that you both respect each other's viewpoints and continue to communicate openly.

Talking to adults about puberty doesn't have to feel like navigating a minefield. With the right timing, preparation, and understanding, you can have productive and supportive conversations that help you navigate this changing tide with a bit more ease. Remember, it's about finding common ground, even amidst differing perspectives, and ensuring you have the support you need as you grow.

Friendships: Making and Keeping Them

In the grand tapestry of life, friendships are the vibrant threads that add color, texture, and warmth. They're our confidants in moments of joy, our comfort in times of sorrow, and often, our guides through the maze of growing up. The value of these relationships cannot be overstated, as they provide not only companionship but also a safe space for emotional support and personal growth.

Navigating the waters of making new friends might seem scary, like stepping onto a stage without knowing the dance. Yet, it's in these moments of uncertainty that the most beautiful connections can form. Embarking on the journey of friendship starts with a simple yet profound step: being open to new encounters. Life is full of interesting characters waiting to become part of your story. Whether it's striking up a conversation in class, joining a new club, or volunteering for a cause close to your heart, each new activity is a doorway to potential friendships. The key lies in sharing your genuine self. Authenticity attracts people to each other acting as a beacon for others who resonate with your true essence.

But what about the friendships that already light up your world? Like any living thing, relationships need nurturing to grow.

This might look like:

Regular check-ins: A simple "How are you?" can mean the world. It's these small gestures that knit the fabric of friendship tighter, showing that you care and are there, rain or shine.

Celebrating their wins: From acing a test to mastering a new skateboard trick, rejoice in their victories. Joy shared is joy doubled.

Navigating disagreements with care: Conflicts, while uncomfortable, are inevitable. Approach them with the intent to understand, not to win. A resolution reached together strengthens the bond.

Not all relationships are good for us. Recognizing when a friendship is no longer good for our well-being is important for emotional health. These are connections that leave you feeling drained, devalued, or disrespected.

Signs to watch for include:

One-sided effort: You're always the one making plans, reaching out, or offering support.

Disrespect for boundaries: Your expressed needs and limits are ignored or ridiculed.

Constant negativity: Interactions are filled with criticism, jealousy, or pessimism, overshadowing the joy of companionship. When faced with such patterns, setting boundaries or, in some cases, letting go becomes an act of self-care. It's not about harboring ill will but about prioritizing your peace and growth. Sometimes, the most loving thing we can do for ourselves and others is to walk away from relationships that no longer serve us.

Friendships, in all their complexity, are some of life's most precious gifts. They mirror our evolution, growing as we do, reflecting our joys, sorrows, and all of the different experiences in between. As you go about your life, remember that the quality of the threads you choose Through the friendships you nurture you can turn each friendship into a masterpiece of connection, support, and shared happiness.

Bullying: How to Stand Up for Yourself and Others

Imagine walking down a hallway filled with laughter, chatter, and the occasional dropped book. This is where friendships bloom, ideas form, and memories are made. Yet, for some, this same hallway feels like navigating a minefield, where every corner could hide a harsh word or unkind action. Yes, we're talking about bullying - a reality far too many face. Understanding it, standing up to it, and supporting those in its path are steps we all need to take.

Understanding Bullying

Bullying isn't just a push in the playground or an eye roll in class. It's a pattern of behavior where someone intentionally and repeatedly causes discomfort or harm to another person.

Bullying can morph into different forms:

Physical Bullying: This involves physical harm or threats of violence.

Verbal Bullying: It includes name-calling, teasing, or making nasty comments. Even if you're joking, you need to think about your words before you speak out loud. Just because you find something funny to laugh at, it doesn't mean that it has to be said.

Cyberbullying: A digital era menace, where bullies use social media, texts, or emails to intimidate or harass people.

Each form leaves scars, some visible, others hidden deep within, affecting self-esteem, academic performance, and emotional wellbeing.

Strategies to Stand Up to Bullying

Facing a bully might feel like standing at the edge of a cliff, but remember, you're not alone, and you're stronger than you think.

Here are strategies to reclaim your power and stand tall:

Assertiveness (or bold self-confidence) training: Learning to express yourself confidently and calmly can disarm a bully. Practice stating your needs and standing your ground in safe environments.

Seeking help from adults: It's not tattling; it's taking control. Teachers, parents, and counselors can offer support and intervene when necessary.

The buddy system: Bullies often target those who are alone. Sticking with friends can provide a shield of solidarity against bullying attempts.

Supporting Others

If you see someone being bullied, remember, your voice can be their shield. **Your actions can make a world of difference:**

Offer comfort: Sometimes, just being there can help someone feel less isolated. Listen to them, affirm their feelings, and remind them that they're not alone.

Report bullying: If you witness bullying, speak up. Whether it's to a teacher, a school counselor, or another adult, your voice can initiate change.

Promote a culture of kindness: Challenge the status quo by being an example of kindness and inclusion. Start initiatives that celebrate diversity and encourage empathy.

Building Resilience

In the face of bullying, resilience is your armor. It's about bouncing back stronger, with the knowledge that you are more than the words or actions thrown at you.

Here's how to fortify your spirit:

Self-care: Nurturing your physical and emotional wellbeing can boost your resilience. Whether it's through exercise, hobbies, or relaxation techniques, find what replenishes your strength.

Positive self-talk: Replace the bully's narrative with your own voice of kindness and affirmation. Remind yourself of your worth, your strengths, and your right to be treated with respect.

Seeking support: Surround yourself with people who uplift you. Friends, family, and support groups can offer the comfort and encouragement needed to navigate through tough times.

Standing up to bullying is not just about confrontations. It's about creating an environment where everyone feels safe, valued, and respected. It's about turning the hallway from a place of fear into a space where every step is taken with confidence, knowing that you have the tools and the community to support you. Remember, your voice has the power to change the narrative, not just for you, but for everyone around you.

Online Safety: Navigating Social Media Responsibly

Navigating the digital world is a bit like exploring a vast, bustling city. It's filled with exciting places to visit, interesting people to meet, and endless opportunities to learn and grow. However, just like any big city, it also has its share of risks and areas where you need to tread carefully. In the realm of social media, understanding how to move through this space safely and responsibly is key to making the most of its benefits while avoiding potential pitfalls.

Digital Footprint Awareness

Every comment you post, photo you share, or profile you visit leaves a trace in the digital landscape, much like footprints in the sand. Over time, these traces accumulate into what's known as your digital footprint—a lasting record of your online activities. It's crucial to be mindful of the footprints you're leaving behind, as they can have long-term implications. Future employers, college admissions officers, and even potential friends might one day walk through the paths you've left, forming impressions based on what they find.

Here are some important tips:

Think before you post: Pause and consider the potential impact of your words or images. Ask yourself, "Is this something I'd be comfortable with everyone seeing, now and years down the line?"

Regularly review your online presence: Periodically go through your social media profiles and remove or privatize posts that don't represent who you are or who you want to be.

Privacy Settings and Personal Information

Social media platforms have different tools and settings that are designed to give you control over who sees your content and how your information is shared online. But these tools can only protect you if you know how to use them correctly.

Dive into the privacy settings: Familiarize yourself with the privacy options on each social media platform you use. Adjust your settings to limit who can see your posts, contact you, or find your profile through searches.

Be cautious with personal information: Avoid sharing details that could be used to identify or locate you, such as your home address, phone number, or even your school's name. It's like giving out a key to your personal world; make sure it's only in the right hands.

Dealing with Online Harassment

The disguise of not knowing who people are can sometimes encourage individuals to act unkindly or aggressively online. If you find yourself getting online harassment or cyberbullying, remember that you're not powerless. There are steps you can take to avoid online harassment and cyberbullying.

Block and report: Most social media platforms have mechanisms for blocking users and reporting abusive behavior. Utilizing these tools correctly can help create a safer online environment for you and others.

Seek support: Don't hesitate to talk to a trusted adult about what you're experiencing. They can offer guidance, support, and sometimes intervene on your behalf.

Document the abuse: Keeping a record of harassing, bullying and mean messages or posts. Taking those steps can be useful if the situation escalates and you need to involve authorities or platform moderators.

Positive Online Interactions

While it's important to be aware of the risks, it's equally important to remember that social media can be a powerful tool for positive connections and self-expression. It's a platform where you can share your passions, celebrate achievements, and connect with others who share your interests.

Contribute to positive spaces: Engage in communities and groups that focus on uplifting content, support, and shared interests. Your voice can add value and encourage others.

Be a force for kindness: Compliment someone's work, offer support during tough times, or share resources that could help others. Small acts of kindness can ripple through the online world, making it a brighter place for everyone.

Express yourself creatively: Use social media as a canvas to share your art, ideas, and stories. It's a way to showcase your uniqueness and inspire others.

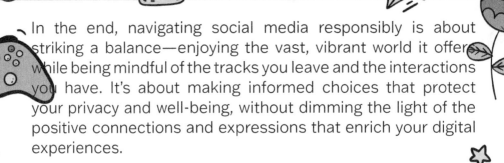

In the end, navigating social media responsibly is about striking a balance—enjoying the vast, vibrant world it offers while being mindful of the tracks you leave and the interactions you have. It's about making informed choices that protect your privacy and well-being, without dimming the light of the positive connections and expressions that enrich your digital experiences.

Peer Pressure: Making Decisions for Yourself

Navigating the social landscape of growing up can sometimes feel like trying to keep your balance on a seesaw. On one side, you have your values and beliefs, and on the other, the weight of peer pressure, tipping you back and forth. Understanding peer pressure, recognizing its forms, and learning how to stay grounded in your sense of self can turn this balancing act into a walk in the park.

Recognizing Peer Pressure

Peer pressure sneaks up in many disguises, sometimes so subtly you might not even notice until you're already feeling its weight. It can be as direct as a friend daring you to skip class, or as indirect as feeling you need to wear certain brands to fit in. Both types play on the desire to belong, making you question your choices.

Direct pressure feels like being put on the spot. It's the unexplainable push to change who you are, even if it's only for a moment, to do what others are doing.

Indirect pressure is trickier; it's the silent nudge from seeing peers act in a certain way, making you feel left out if you don't follow suit.

Staying True to Your Values

Your values are like your personal compass; they guide your

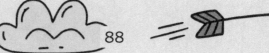

decisions and actions. Keeping them in sight, especially when peer pressure increases, ensures you don't lose your way.

Reflect on what matters most to you. Is it honesty? Kindness? Achievement? Identifying your core values gives you a touchstone to return to when faced with decisions.

Visual reminders can help. A bracelet, a note in your wallet, or a phone wallpaper with a meaningful quote can serve as a prompt to stay aligned with your values.

Confidence Skills

Confidence is your shield and sword when navigating peer pressure. It's about expressing your thoughts and feelings and keeping true to yourself. Without stepping on other's toes.

Practice saying no with conviction. A firm but polite "No thanks" or "That's not for me" shows you're secure in your decisions.

Offering alternatives can soften the blow. If you're uncomfortable with the plan, suggest something else. "I'm not up for that, but how about we go for a pizza instead?"

The Role of Self-Confidence

Self-confidence is the root from which your ability to withstand peer pressure grows. It's your internal sense of assurance, a quiet voice that says, "I know who I am, and I'm okay with that."

Build self-confidence by setting and achieving small goals. Each success, no matter how minor, is a building block for your self-esteem.

Celebrate your uniqueness. Embrace what sets you apart and let go of the notion that you need to change to fit in. Your individuality is your strength.

As you move through the twists and turns of growing up, remember that peer pressure is just one of the many challenges you'll face. Yet, with a strong sense of self, bolstered by your values, assertiveness, and confidence, you can navigate these pressures without losing sight of who you are. These skills aren't just about resisting the urge to change ; they're about creating a life that's authentically yours, filled with choices that reflect your true self.

As we wrap up this exploration of peer pressure and the tools to stand firm against it, remember the importance of listening to your inner voice. It's a conversation that ties back to everything we've discussed about communication, online safety, and friendships.

These are not standalone battles but interconnected parts of your journey. Staying true to yourself, being confident in your needs, and valuing your unique path set the stage for meaningful connections and a fulfilling life ahead. Now, let's turn the page and continue our adventure, equipped with knowledge and a stronger sense of self.

Chapter Five

Seeking Help & Advice

Imagine puberty as a complicated dance routine you've never performed before. Sure, you've seen others do it, and you have maybe even picked up a few moves here and there. But when it's your turn to hit the stage, the steps aren't as easy as they look. Now, think of trusted adults as your behind-the-scenes crew, ready with the right cues, a comforting presence, and sometimes, the necessary push to get you through the performance. This chapter is all about identifying those go-to people and learning how to approach them, ensuring you're never dancing in the dark.

Identifying Trusted Adults and How to Approach Them

Recognizing Trusted Adults

So, who makes the cut as a trusted adult? It's someone you feel safe sharing your thoughts and concerns with, someone who listens without jumping to judgments. This could be a parent, but it could also be a teacher, coach, relative, or even a family friend. Identifying these individuals involves a bit of introspection and observation. Ask yourself: Who do I feel comfortable being around? Who has given me solid advice in the past? Who makes me feel heard? These questions can help you pinpoint the adults in your life who are equipped to offer the support you need.

Look for signs of trustworthiness: Consistency, compassion, and confidentiality are key indicators.

Consider their role in your life: Sometimes, their position or experience can make them particularly good at offering guidance on certain topics.

Approaching Difficult Conversations

Starting a tough conversation can feel as daunting as initiating a chat with your crush—heart-racing, palms sweating. But with the right approach, you can navigate these talks with confidence. **Here's how:**

Choose the right time and place: Go for a quiet, private setting where you won't be interrupted. Timing is crucial too. Maybe after dinner when things have calmed down, or during a weekend morning coffee run.

Plan what you want to say: Organize your thoughts beforehand. You might even write down key points or questions you want to cover.

Express your feelings clearly: Use "I feel" statements to communicate your emotions without placing blame.

Overcoming Hesitation

It's natural to feel hesitant or nervous about opening up. Fear of being misunderstood or dismissed can hold you back. Overcoming this hesitation often begins with reminding yourself of the potential benefits—gaining insights, solutions, or simply unloading some of that emotional weight.

Start small: Share something less sensitive to gauge their response and build your comfort level.

Remind yourself of their care for you: Trusted adults are in your corner. They want to help, even if they might not always know the right things to say or do.

Expecting Diverse Reactions

Not every adult will react the way you anticipate, and that's okay. Some might offer immediate solutions, while others might need time to process what you've shared. Preparing for a range of reactions can help you stay grounded, regardless of the outcome.

Be ready for questions: They might seek more information to understand your situation better.

Stay patient: If their initial reaction isn't what you hoped for, give them time. They might come around once they've had a chance to reflect.

Approaching trusted adults for help or advice can significantly ease the challenges of puberty. Remember, it's about finding someone who respects your feelings, listens with an open heart, and supports you in finding your way. And while starting these conversations might seem scary at first, each step you take towards opening up builds a bridge of understanding, making the next chat a little easier. The right support can turn the trickiest dance routines of puberty into a performance you're proud to call your own.

Resources and Where to Find Reliable Information

There are so many paths to take and sights to see, but it's easy to feel lost. That's why having a guidebook, in the form of credible information, can make all the difference. Here's how to sift through the mountains of advice, facts, and opinions to find the treasure trove of reliable, helpful information.

Evaluating Sources

The internet is a jungle of information where truth and fiction often intertwine. Learning to distinguish between these is like developing a superpower. **Here are some tips to enhance your info-sleuthing abilities:**

Look for expertise: Check if the information comes from professionals or organizations with credentials you can verify. A health website endorsed by doctors or institutions is more reliable than a random blog post.

Check the date: With science and understanding constantly evolving, ensuring the information is up-to-date is crucial. Something written ten years ago might not hold true today.

Cross-reference: Don't rely on a single source. Cross-checking facts across multiple reputable platforms can help confirm their accuracy.

Recommended Resources

To save you some legwork, we've put together a starter kit of resources known for their credibility and user-friendly information on puberty.

For straight-up facts: The Centers for Disease Control and Prevention (CDC) offers a wealth of health-related information that's regularly updated.

Interactive learning: Amaze.org provides engaging, animated videos that cover everything puberty-related without making you bored or yawn.

Books galore: "The Care and Keeping of You" series by American Girl is a gem for navigating physical and emotional changes. For the boys, "Guy Stuff: The Body Book for Boys" offers similar guidance.

Community wisdom: Scarleteen.com is an inclusive, comprehensive resource for all questions puberty and beyond, offering advice through articles, , Q&As, which are questions and answers and forums

Remember, while these resources are a great starting point, they're just part of the learning journey. Keep exploring, asking questions, and seeking out new sources of information.

Staying Informed

Keeping up with the latest can be as easy as subscribing to a newsletter or joining an online forum.

Here's how to stay in the loop:

Sign up for newsletters from trusted health organizations. It's like getting a regular digest of all things puberty and health, delivered straight to your inbox."

Workshops and webinars can be goldmines of information. Look out for local health organizations or schools hosting these events.

Online forums and discussion groups offer a space to ask questions and share experiences. Just make sure the community is moderated to keep the conversation respectful and informative.

Privacy and Safety Online

While the internet is an incredible resource, it's also a place where privacy and safety should never be taken lightly.

Here are some golden rules to follow:

Keep personal info personal: Avoid sharing details like your full name, address, or school. It's like giving out a key to your privacy.

Secure your accounts: Use strong, unique passwords for each of your social media or forum accounts. It's like locking your diary with a key only you know.

Think before you click: If a website asks for too much personal information or something feels off, trust your gut. Not every site is a safe place to wander.

Armed with these guidelines, you're now set to navigate the vast seas of puberty information with confidence. Remember, while the internet and books can offer a wealth of knowledge, nothing beats talking to a healthcare provider or trusted adult for advice tailored specifically to you.

How to Start Conversations with Parents About Puberty

Navigating the conversation about puberty with your parents can feel like you're about to step on stage without knowing your lines. Yep, it's that mix of anticipation and butterflies in your belly. But, hey, every great performance starts with breaking the ice, right? So, let's get you prepped and ready to have that talk, making it less about stage fright and more about sharing the spotlight.

Breaking the Ice

Finding the perfect opener can turn a daunting dialogue into a smooth convo. **Consider these icebreakers as your opening act:**

Share a related story: Maybe it's something funny or awkward that happened at school, or a scene from a movie you watched. It's a natural way to steer the conversation towards puberty without the spotlight solely on you.

Ask for their story: Flip the script and ask them about their experiences. It's a gentle door-opener, showing you're interested in their journey too, which can make them more open to discussing yours.

Expressing Needs and Concerns

Once the ice is shattered, it's showtime—time to share what's on your mind. **Here's how to ensure your message gets a standing ovation:**

Be clear and direct: Dancing around the topic can lead to misunderstandings. If you're worried about acne or curious about emotional changes, say so. Clarity is key.

Speak from the heart: Let them know why this conversation is important to you. Maybe you're feeling anxious, curious, or just plain confused. Sharing from a place of honesty invites empathy and understanding.

Ask for what you need: Whether it's advice, a trip to the doctor, or just someone to listen, being specific about what you're seeking helps them understand how they can support you.

Using Resources as Conversation Aids

Sometimes, having a visual or textual prop can make all the difference, serving as a supporting character in your talk:

Bring a book or article: If you've found a helpful resource, share it with them. It can be a great way to introduce topics you're unsure how to tackle alone.

Use educational videos: Watching a video together can break the tension and provide a starting point for discussion. Plus, it shows you're coming from a place of wanting to learn.

Navigating Disagreements or Discomfort

Even with the best-laid plans, you might hit a bump or two. **Here's how to keep the conversation rolling:**

Stay calm and respectful: If your parents seem taken aback or disagree with something, keep your cool. Remember, this might be new topic for them too.

Agree to revisit: If it's clear the conversation isn't going anywhere productive, it's okay to pause and suggest talking about it another time.

Find another confidant: Sometimes, you might need to seek advice elsewhere. This doesn't mean giving up on talking to your parents, but rather, widening your support network. Figure out who else you can talk to about puberty.

Tackling the topic of puberty with your parents doesn't have to feel like a solo act on a big stage. With the right approach, you can turn it into a collaborative performance, where everyone's experiences and insights contribute to the story. . Remember, it's about opening the lines of communication, sharing your journey, and seeking the support you need as you navigate the ups and downs of growing up.

Support Groups and Clubs: Finding Your Community

Finding your tribe or your community during the whirlwind of puberty can feel a bit like trying to catch fireflies on a summer night. It's magical when you do, but boy, does it require some patience and strategy. Support groups and clubs are like jars for those fireflies—spaces where you can gather with others who light up your world in unique ways, offering shared experiences, mutual support, and a chance to form new friendships. Let's explore how these groups can light up different corners of your world and how you can find or even create one that fits just right.

The Glow of Joining Support Groups

Imagine walking into a room (or logging into Facebook, Instagram or Twitter) where everyone gets it. They understand the ups, the downs, and the sideways slides of puberty because they're right there with you. That's the importance of a support group.

Here's what makes them important :

Shared experiences mean you're not alone. Hearing others' stories can be a balm to the soul, offering both relief and a sense of belonging.

Mutual support is the backbone of these groups. Whether it's advice on handling stress or just a listening ear, the give-and-take of support weaves strong bonds.

Making new friends who are on similar paths can add bright new colors to your social circle, enriching your life in unexpected ways.

Lighting the Way to the Right Group

Finding the group that feels like home to you can take a bit of searching, but when you find it, you'll know.

Here are some ideas to guide your way:

Reflect on what you need. Is it a space to talk about the emotional rollercoaster of puberty, or are you looking for folks who share a specific interest or identity? Knowing what you're seeking can narrow down the search.

School clubs and community centers are great starting points. They often host a variety of groups, from art clubs to offering safe spaces to explore interests and identities.

Illuminating Your Participation

Once you've found a group that feels like a good fit, diving in actively can help you reap the most benefits. Think of it as not just catching those fireflies but also learning about their glow. **Here's how to make the most of your group:**

Regular attendance helps build familiarity and trust. It's like watering a plant; consistent care fosters growth.

Engage in discussions, even if it's just to share a small insight or offer support to someone else. Your voice adds to the group's tapestry, enriching the experience for everyone.

Volunteering for activities or to help organize meetings can deepen your connection to the group and its members. It's a chance to contribute your unique light to the collective glow.

Crafting Your Own Constellation

Sometimes, despite all your searching, you might not find a group that fits just right. When that happens, why not create your own?

Here's a flashlight to guide you through the process:

Identify the focus of your group. Will it be a general puberty support group or centered around a specific interest or aspect of growing up?

Spread the word in a way that reaches your intended members. School bulletins, community center notice boards, or social media platforms can be effective channels. Organizing the first meeting might feel daunting, but keeping it simple can ease the pressure. A get-to-know-you session with some icebreakers can set a welcoming tone.

Facilitating discussions ensures everyone's voice is heard. Prepare a few topics or questions in advance to keep the conversation flowing.

In the dance of growing up, support groups and clubs can be your rhythm, keeping you moving even when the steps get tricky. Whether you find a group that feels like home or decide to start your own, the connections you make can light up your path through puberty, offering laughter, understanding, and a shared journey through this buzzing, blooming, bewildering time.

When to Seek Professional Help

Sometimes, the road through puberty feels like an obstacle course you never signed up for. It's twisty, turning, and every so often, you stumble upon a hurdle that feels a little too high to jump on your own. That's when ringing in the experts – therapists, counselors, and doctors – becomes not just a smart move, but a brave one.

Spotting the Signs

Imagine you're on a hike, and suddenly, the weather changes. Just like you'd recognize storm clouds rolling in, it's crucial to

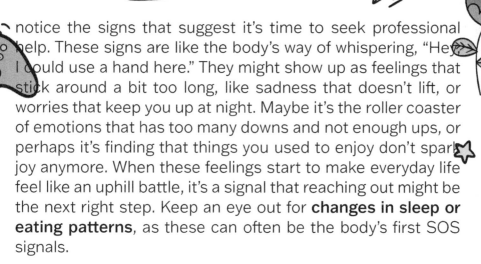

notice the signs that suggest it's time to seek professional help. These signs are like the body's way of whispering, "Hey, I could use a hand here." They might show up as feelings that stick around a bit too long, like sadness that doesn't lift, or worries that keep you up at night. Maybe it's the roller coaster of emotions that has too many downs and not enough ups, or perhaps it's finding that things you used to enjoy don't spark joy anymore. When these feelings start to make everyday life feel like an uphill battle, it's a signal that reaching out might be the next right step. Keep an eye out for **changes in sleep or eating patterns**, as these can often be the body's first SOS signals.

Notice if school, friendships, or hobbies start to feel more like burdens than pleasures.

Navigating the World of Support

Think of the realm of professional help as a garden, lush with different plants, each with its unique way of providing shade or color. In this garden, various professionals are ready to offer support, each bringing their expertise to the table.

Counselors and therapists are like the guiding paths in the garden, helping you navigate your feelings and thoughts, offering strategies to cope with the emotional mazes of puberty.

Pediatricians and family doctors are similar to the gardeners, and they make sure your physical health is on track, addressing any bodily changes or concerns that puberty throws your way. **School nurses and psychologists** act as the benches in the garden, offering a moment of rest and support, right where you are.

Preparing for the Consultation

Walking into a professional's office can feel scary, like stepping onto a stage. But a little preparation can turn this into a conversation rather than an interrogation.

Write down what you've been feeling and experiencing. Putting it on paper can help you organize your thoughts and ensure you cover everything you want to discuss.

List any questions you have. It's easy to forget in the moment, so having them written down can be a big help.

Remember, no concern is too big or too small. If it matters to you, it's worth mentioning.

Embracing the Step Forward

Seeking help often comes with its own set of worries, thanks in part to the old tales of stigma that society has created around mental and emotional health. Yet, taking this step is about strength, not weakness. It's acknowledging that you're not meant to walk this path alone and that asking for help is part of taking care of yourself.

Remember, feelings are just visitors; they come and go. Seeking help is about learning how to be a good host.

Everyone's experience with puberty is unique, and reaching out for support is a personalized part of that journey.

As we wrap up, it's clear that navigating the challenges of puberty sometimes means calling in reinforcements. Whether it's the emotional whirlwinds, the physical puzzles, or just feeling a bit lost in the woods, there's a world of support waiting to lend a hand. Recognizing when you need that extra help, understanding who's out there ready to provide it, and preparing to make the most of their expertise are all steps towards not just surviving puberty, but thriving through it. And remember, seeking help isn't a detour; it's part of the path forward, a sign of taking charge of your journey. So, as we move forward, let's carry this mindset with us, ready to embrace the adventures and challenges ahead with confidence and courage.

Chapter Six

Unique Challenges & Celebrations

Imagine puberty puberty as a puzzle where every piece fits differently for each person. Now, add another layer to this puzzle for tweens with disabilities. The picture on the box might look similar, but the pieces might need a bit of customization to fit perfectly. This chapter shines a light on the unique challenges tweens with disabilities face during puberty and how to navigate these with grace, understanding, and a bit of creativity.

Understanding Diverse Experiences

No two puberty experiences are the same. For tweens with disabilities, puberty can feel like playing a video game where the rules aren't entirely clear, or the controller works a bit differently. Physical changes are one thing, but when you factor in a disability, whether it's a mobility issue, a neurological condition, or a sensory impairment, the usual advice doesn't always apply directly. It's crucial to recognize and embrace these differences, not as hurdles but as unique aspects of the journey.

Physical changes might be more challenging or require special attention: For instance, a tween in a wheelchair might need different strategies for managing menstruation comfortably and privately.

Emotional and social changes could have added layers: Tweens with disabilities might feel more isolated or misunderstood by their peers. They might wonder how their changing bodies will affect their independence or how others perceive them.

Adapting Self-Care Routines

Self-care during puberty, from managing hygiene to understanding bodily changes, can require some out-of-the-box thinking for tweens with disabilities. It's about finding what works for you, which might mean adapting tools or routines to fit your needs.

Hygiene aids: There are tools designed for easier use, like adapted nail clippers or no-rinse bathing wipes, that can make personal care more accessible.

Clothing adaptations: For those with sensory issues, puberty means not just new sizes but also dealing with textures and fits that feel comfortable. Brands now cater to a wide range of sensory needs with seamless, tag-free, and soft clothing options.

Period products: There are more choices than ever, from period underwear to menstrual, period cups, offering options that might be easier to use depending on your mobility or comfort level.

Seeking Tailored Resources and Support

Finding resources and support that address the intersection of puberty and disability can make a world of difference. It's about seeing yourself in the advice given and the stories told.

Specialized healthcare providers: Look for doctors, therapists, or counselors who understand both puberty and disability. They can offer personalized advice and solutions.

Support groups: Online forums or local groups can connect you with other tweens who share similar experiences. It's a space to exchange tips, vent about frustrations, or celebrate successes.

Educational resources: Seek out books, websites, or videos that include perspectives on puberty from people with disabilities. Representation matters, especially when navigating something as complex as puberty.

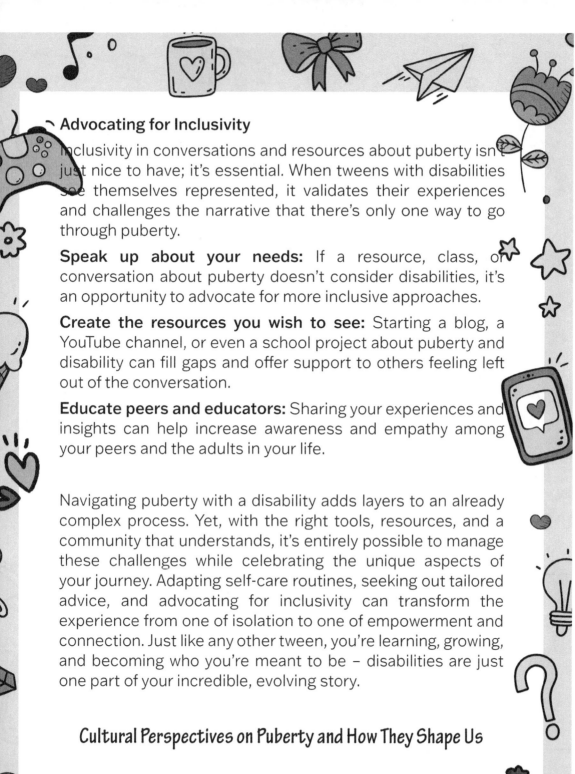

Advocating for Inclusivity

Inclusivity in conversations and resources about puberty isn't just nice to have; it's essential. When tweens with disabilities see themselves represented, it validates their experiences and challenges the narrative that there's only one way to go through puberty.

Speak up about your needs: If a resource, class, or conversation about puberty doesn't consider disabilities, it's an opportunity to advocate for more inclusive approaches.

Create the resources you wish to see: Starting a blog, a YouTube channel, or even a school project about puberty and disability can fill gaps and offer support to others feeling left out of the conversation.

Educate peers and educators: Sharing your experiences and insights can help increase awareness and empathy among your peers and the adults in your life.

Navigating puberty with a disability adds layers to an already complex process. Yet, with the right tools, resources, and a community that understands, it's entirely possible to manage these challenges while celebrating the unique aspects of your journey. Adapting self-care routines, seeking out tailored advice, and advocating for inclusivity can transform the experience from one of isolation to one of empowerment and connection. Just like any other tween, you're learning, growing, and becoming who you're meant to be – disabilities are just one part of your incredible, evolving story.

Cultural Perspectives on Puberty and How They Shape Us

Puberty, a universal experience, is painted with the unique brushstrokes of various cultures around the globe. It's like opening a vast book filled with stories from every corner of the world, each chapter revealing how different societies

understand and celebrate this significant life phase. This rich tapestry of traditions and beliefs offers a colorful backdrop against which you can explore your own puberty experience.

Exploring Cultural Diversity

In some cultures, the onset of puberty is marked with grand ceremonies and rituals. For example, consider the Latin American Quinceañera or the Japanese Seijin Shiki, each a rite of passage that acknowledges and celebrates the transition from childhood to adulthood. These traditions not only honor the individual but also reinforce community bonds. Other cultures might approach puberty with more subtlety, focusing on education and mentorship to guide the young person through their transformation. By looking at this wide array of customs, we see a world that values and recognizes puberty in many beautiful, elaborate, or even pragmatic ways. This exploration helps us appreciate the diversity of human experience and encourages us to see our own puberty journey in a broader, more connected context.

Respecting Cultural Practices

Honoring our cultural practices related to puberty while also being open to learning about and from the experiences of others enriches our understanding of this life stage. It's like putting together different threads to create a more intricate, detailed, and inclusive narrative. For those of us with a rich cultural heritage, and participating in traditional ceremonies or practices can deepen our connection to our roots and ancestors. While at the same time, it allows us to continue showing genuine curiosity and respect for how others navigate puberty. All of this fosters a sense of global relationships and mutual respect.

Navigating Cultural and Personal Beliefs

At times, our personal feelings about puberty or our individual experiences may not entirely align with our cultural or familial expectations. This mismatch can feel like trying to play a melody in harmony with an orchestra, only to find your instrument slightly out of tune. It's a delicate dance, finding a way to honor your cultural background while also staying true to your personal journey. Open communication is key here. Engaging in honest discussions with family members or community elders about your feelings and experiences can open the door to a more nuanced understanding on both sides. In some cases, you might find ways to adapt traditional practices to better fit your needs or create new rituals that resonate more deeply with your personal experience of puberty.

Celebrating Cultural Identity

Our cultural identity shapes not just how we experience puberty but also how we view ourselves and our place in the world. It's a lens through which we interpret our changing bodies and emotions. Embracing this aspect of our identity can be a source of strength and pride. Celebrating the unique way your culture approaches puberty can help you feel more grounded and connected during this transformative time. Whether it's by participating in traditional ceremonies, learning about the puberty rites of your ancestors, or simply talking with family members about their own experiences, these acts of celebration and connection remind us that puberty is not just a biological milestone but also a deeply cultural one.

In a world that often seeks to generalize or simplify, acknowledging and honoring the complex interplay of cultural perspectives on puberty is a powerful act of self-discovery and respect. It reminds us that while the physical and emotional changes of puberty are universal, the ways in which we navigate, understand, and celebrate these changes are as diverse as humanity itself. By exploring and respecting this diversity, we not only enrich our own puberty experience but also deepen our appreciation for the rich tapestry of human culture and tradition.

The Role of Creativity and Hobbies in Emotional Health

When the waves of puberty seem to crash in from all sides, finding an anchor in creativity and hobbies isn't just fun—it's a much-needed lifeline. Picture this: each brush stroke on a canvas, each note in a melody, or each step in a dance routine can be a step away from stress toward serenity and calmness. Now, let's explore how these acts of creation and participation in activities we love can be a soothing balm for the roller coaster of emotions that puberty often brings.

A Symphony of Well-being

Imagine your emotional health as a complicated symphony, with each instrument playing an important role in creating harmony. Creative activities and hobbies act as the conductors, ensuring each section comes in at the right time and maintaining balance and beauty in the composition. Whether it's painting, writing, coding, or playing sports, these activities offer a unique blend of benefits.

Stress relief: Engaging in something you're passionate about can shift your focus away from worries and immerse you in the joy of the moment.

Self-expression: Creativity offers a voice when words fall short, allowing feelings to flow through art, music, crafts, or movement.

Confidence boost: Mastering a new chord on the guitar or nailing a complicated move in a dance routine reinforces the belief in your abilities, lighting up the path to self-confidence.

Diverse Explorations

The world of hobbies and creative outlets is as vast and varied as the stars in the night sky. Each one holds the potential to ignite a spark of interest that could grow into a blazing passion.

Here's why casting a wide net and trying a lot of activities can be especially rewarding for you during puberty:

New discoveries: You might stumble upon a hobby you never considered before, one that brings you a lot of joy calmness and peace.

Skill development: Dabbling in different interests not only broadens your horizons but also allows you to hone skills that can be valuable in other areas of your life.

Adaptability: As you grow and change, your interests might change too. What starts as a casual curiosity could evolve into a lifelong passion or future career path.

Creative Coping

When the emotional skies of puberty darken, turning to creative outlets and hobbies can be like opening an umbrella of resilience. **Here are some ways creativity serves as a coping mechanism:**

Journaling: Writing down your thoughts and feelings can declutter your mind and offer new perspectives on what you're experiencing.

Art therapy: Drawing, painting, or sculpting provides a tangible way to process emotions, often revealing insights and solutions that were hidden beneath the surface.

Physical activity: Sports, dance, or even just a walk while listening to music can elevate mood, reduce stress, and increase energy levels.

Community and Connection

Beyond the personal benefits, hobbies and creative activities often lead to the discovery of a community of like-minded individuals. **These connections can create a safety net of support, understanding, and shared joy:**

Clubs and groups: Joining a club, whether at school or in the community, dedicated to your interest area can introduce you to friends who 'get it'.

Online communities: There are forums, social media groups, and websites where you can share your work, get feedback, and connect with others from around the globe.

Events and competitions: Participating in events like art shows, music competitions, or sports matches can increase sense of belonging and team spirit.

In the grand tapestry of growing up, intertwining threads of creativity and hobbies add depth, color, and strength, helping to navigate the complex emotions and changes of puberty. From the calming rhythm of strumming a guitar to the focused calm of coding a new app or the exhilarating rush of scoring a goal, these activities offer a sanctuary and a safe space of self-expression and joy. They remind us that even in the midst of change, there are constant sources of happiness, growth, and connection. And it's in these spaces that we often find not just solace but ourselves, too.

Technology and Puberty: The Digital Age's Influence

In a world where screens light up our faces more often than the sun, navigating puberty amidst the glow of technology is reality for today's tweens. The digital landscape is vast, offering a blend of information, social connections, and creative outlets that previous generations couldn't have imagined during their puberty years. From the endless scrolls of social media to the boundless resources available online, technology shapes the puberty experience in ways that are profoundly different and inherently modern.

Understanding the Digital Landscape

The digital age brings a wealth of information on puberty, readily available at the touch of a button or the swipe of a screen. Gone are the days of awkwardly searching for answers in library books; now, questions about physical changes, emotional fluctuations, and everything in between can be answered with a quick online search. However, this ease of access also means tweens are bombarded with a dizzying array of voices and perspectives, making it challenging for them to figure out what's helpful and what's not. Social media platforms and online communities offer spaces where tweens can connect, share experiences, and find support from peers going through similar changes. Yet, these digital gathering spots also present new challenges, from the pressure to present a perfect image to the world to navigating the complexities of online interactions.

Navigating Digital Challenges

For all its benefits, the digital world can be a tricky landscape to navigate during puberty. The constant stream of images and updates from peers can lead to unhealthy comparisons, where your changing body or emotional experiences feel lacking or abnormal. Cyberbullying introduces a layer of potential harm, where words and actions online can deeply affect your self-esteem and mental health. Information overload is another challenge, where the sheer volume of available advice can overwhelm you rather than enlighten you.

Strategies for healthy digital consumption include:

Taking regular breaks from screens to engage in offline activities and foster real-world connections.

Curating a positive digital environment by following accounts that uplift and educate, rather than those that provoke comparison or negativity.

Discussing experiences of online interactions with trusted adults or peers to get their perspective and support.

Leveraging Technology Positively

Despite its pitfalls, technology offers incredible opportunities for tweens navigating puberty. Online platforms can serve as valuable resources for learning about the physical and emotional aspects of puberty in a safe and anonymous way. Educational websites, guided by experts, offer accurate and age-appropriate information that can empower tweens with knowledge and confidence.

Creative expression finds a new frontier online, where tweens can explore their identities and share their experiences through blogging, vlogging, or digital art. These outlets not only provide a sense of accomplishment but also connect individuals with like-minded communities that celebrate diversity and individuality.

Supportive online communities can be lifelines for tweens who feel isolated or misunderstood in their offline lives. Forums and social media groups dedicated to specific interests or challenges offer spaces where questions can be asked and experiences shared without fear of judgment.

Promoting Digital Literacy and Safety

As the digital landscape becomes an important part of the puberty experience, promoting digital literacy and safety is crucial. Understanding privacy settings on social media platforms, recognizing credible sources of information, and knowing how to protect personal information are critical skills for tweens in the digital age.

Encouraging critical thinking about the content that is consumed online helps tweens become discerning digital citizens, able to navigate the vast sea of information with a clear eye for what's helpful, harmful, or irrelevant.

Finding balance and meaning in the digital age is a key part of navigating puberty today in a world that's increasingly connected through pixels, pictures, and data. Technology offers tools for learning, connecting, and creating in ways that can enrich the puberty experience, provided tweens are equipped with the knowledge and skills to use it wisely and safely.

As we wrap up this exploration of technology's role in puberty, we're reminded of the power and potential that digital tools hold. Used thoughtfully, they can illuminate the path through puberty, offering resources, connections, and outlets for expression that support and enrich the journey. The digital landscape, with all its challenges and opportunities, is a significant part of growing up today, shaping how tweens learn about themselves and the world around them. As we move forward, embracing the positive aspects of technology while fostering digital literacy and safety will continue to be key themes in navigating the complexities of puberty in the modern world.

CONCLUSION

Well, here we are at the end of this wild ride called puberty. Let's take a moment to breathe in, breathe out, and give ourselves a big high-five for making it through. This journey, with all its twists and turns, zits and growth spurts, is nothing short of a rollercoaster—a beautifully complex one that transforms tween girls into... well, slightly older and wiser tween girls.

We've covered a lot, haven't we? From the ABCs of puberty (hello, breasts, also known as boobs, and periods!) to the XYZs of self-care, emotional whirlwinds, and the art of rocking those social skills. We've dived into the nitty-gritty of staying clean and smelling fresh, managing those mood swings like a boss, and finding our squad who'll support us through these crazy years. And let's not forget about seeking out those wise owls in our lives—be it parents, guardians, or that cool aunt who always keeps it real—for guidance and support when the going gets tough.

The big vision here? My mission is to empower you to get through puberty with all the knowledge, confidence, and grace of a queen. Remember, it's all about embracing those changes, understanding your body is doing exactly what it's supposed to do, and reminding yourself that you're pretty awesome for navigating this whole puberty thing with such gusto.

Now, my dear readers, I urge you to keep those lines of communication wide open. Don't be afraid to talk with your parents, your friends, maybe even your pet hamster, or you dog about what's going on with you. Share your stories, lean on each other, and never be afraid to ask for advice or lend an ear to someone in need.

And hey, don't stop here. Keep on exploring, questioning, and learning about this incredible body of yours. Puberty is just the opening act in the grand play of adolescence. Approach each scene with curiosity, an open mind, and maybe a healthy dose of humor because, trust me, laughter makes everything a tad easier.

To the amazing support networks out there—families, friends, teachers, and yes, even those embarrassing parents (I see you, and I've been there)—you play a starring role in this adventure. Keep the dialogue flowing, educate yourselves, and most importantly, shower your tween with empathy and understanding.

So, as we wrap up this guidebook to puberty, let's celebrate this incredible journey of growth, self-discovery, and empowerment. Remember, with the right mix of knowledge, love, and support, you can navigate these tumultuous years with your head held high and a smile on your face.

And to you, brave and beautiful readers: Embrace your journey with every fiber of your being. View each change, each challenge, as an opportunity to grow stronger, wiser, and more in tune with the amazing person you're destined to become. Approach your evolving body and shifting emotions with kindness, pride, and a dash of wonder. Because, in the grand scheme of things, puberty is not just about growing up—it's about blossoming into the phenomenal individual you are meant to be.

Here's to you, to puberty, and to the incredible journey ahead. You've got this!

Your friend,
Molly x

The Next Chapter is for Your Parents/Adults

Chapter Seven

SUPPORTING YOUR TWEEN THROUGH PUBERTY

Imagine finding yourself in the middle of a bustling city you've never visited before. The streets are filled with unknown faces, the signs are in a language you barely understand, and the map you hold seems to have been drawn for a completely different place. This is often what puberty feels like for tweens - a whirlwind of changes, emotions, and questions with answers that seem just out of reach. Now, picture yourself not as the traveler but as the local - someone who knows the lay of the land, understands the language, and can guide a newcomer with ease and confidence. That's the role you're stepping into as you support your tween through puberty.

Understanding Your Tween's Puberty Experience

Empathy is Key

The first step in this journey is empathy. Remember, empathy isn't just about understanding what your tween is going through; it's about connecting with their feelings. Imagine their frustration when they can't control their emotions or confusion over their physical changes. It's like when you're trying to solve a puzzle, but the pieces keep changing shape.

Real-life example: Picture your tween struggling to manage their emotions and reacting in a way that seems over the top. Instead of dismissing their feelings, acknowledge them. Say, "It seems like you're really upset about this. It's perfectly okay to feel this way."

Educate Yourself

The world of puberty hasn't stood still since you navigated it. With advances in science, shifts in societal attitudes, and the omnipresent, also known as ever-present influence of digital media, the landscape has evolved.

Where to start: Look for updated resources on puberty, focusing on current research and diverse experiences. Websites like the American Academy of Pediatrics or books like "It's Perfectly Normal" by Robie H. Harris can offer solid, up-to-date information.

Recognize Individuality

Every tween's experience with puberty is as unique as their fingerprint. While one child might breeze through changes with minimal fuss, another might find the same changes bewildering or even alarming.

Scenario: If one child starts puberty earlier than their peers, they might feel isolated or different. Acknowledge that feeling of being out of sync and reassure them that puberty happens at the right time for them, not according to a universal schedule.

Supporting Emotional Well-being

The emotional rollercoaster of puberty can be just as challenging, if not more so, than the physical changes. Your tween needs a safe space where they can express their feelings without fear of judgment or dismissal.

How to help: Encourage open conversations. Set aside regular times to check in with your tween, maybe during a walk or while doing an activity together, to make it feel more natural. Validate their feelings by saying things like, "It sounds like you're feeling really stressed about this. Want to talk about it?"

5 Ways to Support Your Tween Through Puberty

Listen Actively: Show you're fully engaged by making eye contact and summarizing their points to ensure understanding.

Stay Informed: Keep up with the latest insights and advice on puberty to offer informed support.

Celebrate Individuality: Embrace and affirm your tween's unique journey through puberty without comparison.

Encourage Expression: Provide various outlets for them to express their feelings, whether through art, writing, or conversation.

Offer Reassurance: Regularly reassure your tween that what they're experiencing is normal and you're always there for them.

Empathy Checklist for Parents

- Did you acknowledge your tween's feelings without offering immediate solutions?

- Have you educated yourself on the modern puberty experience?

- Are you avoiding comparisons with siblings, peers, or your own experiences?

- Do you offer regular, judgment-free zones for your tween to express themselves?

- Have you reassured your tween that their feelings and experiences are valid and normal?

Supporting your tween through puberty requires patience, understanding, and a willingness to learn and adapt. By showing empathy, staying informed, recognizing their individuality, and supporting their emotional well-being, you're not just helping them navigate puberty; you're strengthening your bond with them. You're also fostering trust and open communication with each other. Remember, you're their guide in this new stage of their lives. With your support, they can learn to navigate it with confidence.

How to Talk About Sensitive Topics Without Embarrassment

Creating a space where sensitive topics can flow as freely as the usual day-to-day chatter requires a bit of groundwork. It's similar to setting the stage for a play where every actor feels confident in their role, knowing they have the support and understanding of the audience. Here's how to lay down those foundations, ensuring that conversations about puberty are met with openness rather than any awkwardness.

Crafting a Safe Haven for Conversations

Imagine transforming a section of your home into a no-judgment zone, a cozy corner where words feel as comfortable as an old sweater. This is your first step towards having open discussions with your tween about puberty.

Lighten the ambiance with humor. Make your tween laugh with their favorite joke or quote from a movie or TV show. A shared laugh can help relax the atmosphere, making it easier to start talking about more serious topics.

Choose a setting that feels secure and private. A quiet walk, a calm evening at home, or during a drive with just the two of you can provide the right atmosphere for deep conversations.

Set the expectation that this space is a forum for honesty where any question or topic is welcome. Let them know that they don't have to be afraid or insecure to talk to you. Tell them that they can come to you with anything that is on their mind.

Speaking the Language of Puberty

Diving into discussions about puberty without the right terminology is like trying to navigate a foreign city without knowing the language. Clarity and understanding can only come from using the correct terms and clear language.

Introduce terms early on. Familiarity offers comfort, reducing any potential embarrassment from either side.

If you're unsure about specific terms or their meanings, look them up together. It shows them that learning is a lifelong process and it's okay not to have all the answers. It also shows them that you are willing to sit with them right where they are in that stage of their life and that you're willing to learn with them.

Initiating the Conversation

Waiting for the perfect moment to talk about puberty might mean waiting forever. Instead, weave these discussions into the fabric of everyday life, making them as normal as talking about school or friends.

Use media as a springboard. A scene in a movie or a book plot can offer a natural opening to discuss puberty-related themes.

Share your experiences in a way that's relatable. Remember, the goal is to establish a connection with your tween, not to give them a lecture about puberty.

Embracing Your Vulnerability

Feeling a bit uneasy about discussing the birds and the bees? You're not alone. Recognizing and addressing your discomfort head-on can pave the way for more genuine and effective conversations.

Acknowledge your feelings. Admitting to your tween that you're a bit out of your comfort zone can actually draw you two closer together, showing them it's okay to feel vulnerable.

Seek out resources together. This not only helps both of you learn but also takes the pressure off having to know everything.

By laying these foundations, you create an environment where talking about puberty feels as natural as discussing what's for dinner. It's about building trust, fostering understanding, and ensuring your tween knows they have a reliable source of information and a person who wants to support and comfort them as they navigate the complexities of growing up.

Recognizing the Signs of Struggle and How to Help

Navigating puberty isn't just about new physical changes; it's also about the roller coaster of emotions and the sometimes confusing thoughts that come with it. Spotting when your tween is having a tough time with these changes can be like trying to read a book in a dimly lit room.

You know there's a story unfolding, but you need more light to see it clearly. Here's how to shine that light, so you can see when your tween might need a helping hand or a listening ear.

Know the Signs

First up, let's talk about what to look out for. Changes in mood, behavior, or social habits can be subtle hints that your tween is wrestling with something beneath the surface.

Keep an eye out for:

Mood swings that seem more intense or prolonged than usual: It's like their emotional weather changes from sunny to stormy in seconds, without much warning.

Pulling away from friends or family: Picture a turtle retreating into its shell. If your tween suddenly spends more time alone or seems less interested in activities they used to love, it might be a sign that they're struggling with puberty.

Changes in eating or sleeping patterns: Maybe they're eating a lot more or a lot less, or their once-regular sleep schedule has become unpredictable.

Open Lines of Communication

Having open channels of communication is like keeping the doors and windows open on a warm spring day, allowing fresh air to circulate freely.It makes for a healthier, happier home.

Here's how to keep those lines clear:

Regular check-ins: Make it a habit to ask how they're doing in a way that feels casual and non-intrusive. Sometimes, a simple "How was your day?" can lead to unexpected conversations.

Create a judgment-free zone: Let them know they can talk about anything with you without fear of criticism or immediate solutions. Sometimes, they need to vent.

Share your own feelings: Showing your vulnerability can encourage them to open up. Share your challenges and how you deal with them, making it clear that everyone struggles sometimes. Let them know that having struggles is part of what makes us all human. You can also let them know that there is no shame in struggling or admitting that they need help. Admitting that they are struggling physically or emotionally, mentally is often a sign of strength. Let them know that you are proud of them for asking the tough questions and asking for the help they need.

Seeking Professional Support

There might come a time when professional guidance is needed. This doesn't mean you've failed as a parent or guardian; instead, it's acknowledging that some challenges require specialized skills and knowledge.

Here's when and how to seek that support:

When the usual isn't working: If your attempts to help them navigate mood swings, social withdrawal, or behavioral changes aren't making a difference, it might be time to call in a pro.

Choosing the right professional: Look for pediatricians, counselors, or therapists who have experience with tweens. They'll bring not just their expertise, but also an understanding of the unique challenges this age group faces.

Making the first appointment: Approach this step together. Let your tween know why you think it's a good idea, and involve them in the process as much as possible.

Promoting Resilience

Helping your tween build resilience is like teaching them to swim. It equips them with the skills to navigate the sometimes choppy and often unpredictable waters of life with more confidence.

Here's how to help that resilience grow:

Model coping skills: Show them, through your actions, how to handle stress and setbacks. Whether it's taking deep breaths when frustrated, breaking down problems into manageable parts, or finding humor in difficult situations, these are valuable lessons.

Foster a positive self-image: Celebrate their strengths and encourage their interests. Help them see that their value isn't based on their looks, achievements, or popularity but on who they are inside.

Teach healthy stress management: Introduce them to activities that can help manage stress, like physical exercise, creative hobbies, or mindfulness practices. It's about giving them tools they can use when things get tough.

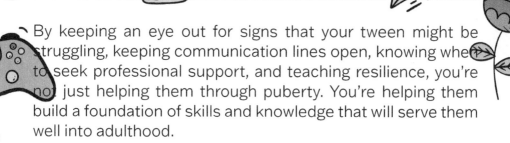

By keeping an eye out for signs that your tween might be struggling, keeping communication lines open, knowing when to seek professional support, and teaching resilience, you're not just helping them through puberty. You're helping them build a foundation of skills and knowledge that will serve them well into adulthood.

Encouraging Independence While Offering Support

Raising a tween through the different stages of puberty is just like teaching them to ride a bike. Initially, you run alongside, gripping the seat to keep them upright. But eventually, you let go, watching as they pedal into newfound freedom, wobbling yet progressing. This delicate dance of offering support while nurturing independence is essential during puberty, a time marked by rapid changes and a quest for self-identity.

Balancing Support and Independence

Finding the sweet spot between being there for your tween and stepping back to let them explore the world is crucial. It's about giving them the room to experience life's ups and downs, knowing you're there to catch them if they fall. This balance teaches resilience, self-reliance, and problem-solving, skills that are essential for adulthood.

Negotiate boundaries together: Sit down and discuss what areas they feel ready to manage on their own and where they might still need guidance. This could range from deciding their own bedtime to choosing their own clothes.

Gradual release of responsibility: Start small, with tasks you feel comfortable letting them handle, like personal hygiene or managing their school assignments. Celebrate their successes and guide them through challenges without taking over.

Teaching Self-Care

Self-care goes beyond the basics of hygiene; it includes managing one's health, emotional well-being, and personal environment. Teaching tweens to take charge of their self-care instills a sense of responsibility and respect for their bodies and minds.

Create a self-care routine together: Make it fun by exploring skincare products or discussing healthy food choices. Incorporate activities that address emotional well-being, like journaling or yoga.

Encourage regular health check-ups: Frame doctor visits not as something to be dreaded and endured but as a proactive step in taking care of their health. Offer to be there with them but give them space to speak directly with the doctor if they want to.

Decision-Making Skills

The ability to make informed decisions about their bodies and health is empowering for tweens navigating puberty. It fosters autonomy and prepares them for the more complex decisions they'll face later on in their lives.

Discuss scenarios: Use everyday situations to discuss potential decisions and their consequences. For example, talk about how to choose healthy snacks or how to respond if they are ever offered a cigarette.

Encourage critical thinking: When they come to you with questions, guide them in researching answers together. It's about teaching them to find reliable information and make choices that align with their values and well-being.

Respecting Privacy

As tweens carve out their identity, privacy becomes a hill they're willing to stand on. Respecting their need for privacy while ensuring that they know you're there for them is the beginning walk of trust and understanding.

Create a safe space: Let them know their room is their sanctuary where they can expect privacy, but also make it clear that you're always available for a chat, no matter the topic no matter the topic they may want to talk to you about.

Use indirect communication: Sometimes, direct conversations can feel too invasive. Leaving notes, sending texts, or sharing articles of interest can be less intrusive ways to communicate, especially on sensitive topics.

Nurturing independence while providing unwavering support equips your tween with the tools they need to navigate puberty with confidence. It's about guiding them to find their own way, make informed choices, and take care of themselves, all while knowing they have a safety net with you as their parent. It's a journey they must ultimately take on their own, but with your guidance, they'll be ready to face it head-on, equipped with the skills, knowledge, and self-assurance to flourish.

Resources for Parents: Books, Websites, and Groups

Navigating the sometimes-turbulent waters of your child's puberty can feel like trying to assemble a puzzle without a picture guide. Thankfully, there are numerous resources are available to not only provide that picture, but also offer pieces that fit just right for your unique situation. Below, you'll find a carefully selected list of resources that can serve as your compass, guiding lights, and anchors as you navigate these transformative years alongside your tween.

Curated Resource List

For those nights when you're scrolling through your phone, looking for answers to the questions your tween just posed, or for the quiet moments when you seek understanding, these resources stand ready to assist:

Books: American Girl's "The Care and Keeping of You" series offers a gentle introduction to the physical changes of puberty, while Frances E. Jensen's "The Teenage Brain" dives into the neurological whirlwind that defines these years.

Websites: The American Academy of Pediatrics (HealthyChildren.org) provides vetted, reliable advice on a wide range of health topics, including puberty. For a broader scope, YourTeenMag.com covers not just the physical but the emotional and social aspects of adolescence.

Apps: AMAZE takes sexual education to a digital platform, offering engaging and informative videos that cover everything puberty-related in a manner that's respectful and age-appropriate.

Community Support

Sometimes, the best guidance comes from those navigating the same waters. Here are ways to connect with others for shared wisdom and support:

Parenting forums: Websites like Circle of Moms and Dad's Corner offer spaces where you can ask questions, share experiences, and receive support from a community of parents worldwide.

Local parent groups: Many communities have parenting groups that meet regularly. These can be a great way to connect, share resources, and find support from those in your geographical area.

School and healthcare seminars: Look for seminars and talks hosted by schools or local healthcare providers. These events can offer valuable insights and connect you with experts in adolescent health.

Professional Resources

At times, the guidance you need goes beyond what books or peer advice can provide.

Here are some pointers on accessing professional resources:

Pediatricians and family doctors: Your child's doctor is often the best starting point for addressing concerns about puberty. They can provide personalized advice and, if needed, referrals to specialists.

Family therapists: For navigating the emotional and relational aspects of puberty, family therapists can offer invaluable support. They can help you and your tween communicate more effectively and work through any challenges that arise.

School counselors: Don't overlook the resources available at your child's school. School counselors are trained to support students through the challenges of adolescence and can be a great ally in ensuring your child's well-being.

Continuous Learning

Staying informed is not a one-time task but a continuous journey. **Here's how to keep learning and stay updated:**

Subscribe to newsletters and podcasts: Look for newsletters from reputable child health and development organizations. Podcasts can also be a great way to receive information and insights while on the go.

Attend workshops and webinars: Many organizations offer workshops and webinars on parenting tweens through puberty. These can be excellent opportunities to learn from experts and ask questions specific to your situation.

Read widely: Keep expanding your library with books and articles on adolescence. The more perspectives you encounter, the richer your understanding and ability to support your tween will be.

As you move forward, equipped with these resources, remember that you're not alone on this journey. From books that break down the basics of puberty to communities of parents sharing their stories, from professional experts offering tailored advice to continuous opportunities for learning, a wealth of support awaits. These resources are your tools, designed to help you provide the best possible guidance and support as your child navigates the complexities of puberty.

With each step, each question answered, and each challenge met with understanding and support, you're not just helping your tween grow through puberty. You're strengthening the bonds of trust and communication that will carry you both through the teenage years and beyond. As we transition from this exploration of resources into the next chapter, let's carry forward the commitment to seeking understanding, fostering open dialogues, and embracing the journey of growth and change together.

REFERENCES

Chavez, M. (2023, August 15). NURTURING YOUNG SKIN: a DERMATOLOGIST'S GUIDE TO PRE-TEEN SKIN CARE. Vitalogy Skincare. https://vitalogyskincare.com/nurturing-young-skin-a-dermatologists-guide-to-pre-teen-skincare/

Choc. (2023, August 25). Puberty: An ultimate guide for parents. CHOC - Children's Health Hub. https://health.choc.org/puberty-an-ultimate-guide-for-parents/

Crompton, K. (2022, August 29). Tech resources that help kids navigate puberty. WIRED. https://www.wired.com/story/tech-resources-kids-puberty/

Department of Health & Human Services. (n.d.). Teenagers and communication. Better Health Channel. https://www.betterhealth.vic.gov.au/health/healthyliving/teenagers-and-communication

Ehmke, R., Steiner-Adair, C., EdD, & Wick, D., EdD. (2023, August 10). How using social media affects teenagers. Child Mind Institute. https://childmind.org/article/how-using-social-media-affects-teenagers/

Garey, J., Rooney, M., PhD, & Steiner-Adair, C., EdD. (2023, November 6). 13 Ways to Boost Your Daughter's Self-Esteem. Child Mind Institute. https://childmind.org/article/13-ways-to-boost-your-daughters-self-esteem/

Healthdirect Australia. (n.d.). Helping your child through puberty. Healthdirect. https://www.healthdirect.gov.au/helping-your-child-through-puberty

How Can Peer Group Influence the Behavior of Adolescents. (n.d.). National Library of Medicine. https://www.ncbi.nlm.nih.gov/pmc/articles/PMC4777050/

Life Challenges and Barriers to Help Seeking: Adolescents. (n.d.). National Library of Medicine. https://www.ncbi.nlm.nih.gov/pmc/articles/PMC8700979/

Morin, A. (2023, November 22). 8 ways to help your middle-schooler connect with other kids. Understood. https://www.understood.org/en/articles/8-ways-to-help-your-middle-schooler-connect-with-other-kids

New Hampshire Family Voices. (2021, October 20). Healthy Bodies - A Parent's Guide on Puberty for Girls with Disabilities - New Hampshire Family Voices. https://nhfv.org/resources/healthy-bodies-parents-guide-puberty-girls-disabilities-2/

Nuñez, C., & Pfeffer, L. (2016a, July 21). 13 Amazing coming of age traditions from around the world. Global Citizen. https://www.globalcitizen.org/en/content/13-amazing-coming-of-age-traditions-from-around-th/

Nuñez, C., & Pfeffer, L. (2016b, July 21). 13 Amazing coming of age traditions from around the world. Global Citizen. https://www.globalcitizen.org/en/content/13-amazing-coming-of-age-traditions-from-around-th/

Nutrition and pubertal development - PMC. (n.d.). National Library of Medicine. https://www.ncbi.nlm.nih.gov/pmc/articles/PMC4266867/

Physical Activity Facts | Healthy Schools | CDC. (n.d.). https://www.cdc.gov/healthyschools/physicalactivity/facts.htm

Robinson, L. (2024, February 5). Cyberbullying: Dealing with Online Bullies. HelpGuide.org. https://www.helpguide.org/articles/abuse/cyberbullying-dealing-online-bullies.htm

Rocker, B. (n.d.). 7 signs your child needs psychological support. https://www.childpsychologist.com.au/resources/7-signs-your-child-needs-psychological-support

Rodriguez, L. (2021, May 27). Which period products are best for the environment? Global Citizen. https://www.globalcitizen.org/en/content/best-period-products-for-the-environment/

Self-Care. (2024, January 30). Kids Helpline. https://kidshelpline.com.au/teens/issues/self-care

Social Media Use and Body Image Disorders: (n.d.). National Library of Medicine. https://www.ncbi.nlm.nih.gov/pmc/articles/PMC8001450/

Suni, E., & Suni, E. (2023, October 4). Teens and sleep. Sleep Foundation. https://www.sleepfoundation.org/teens-and-sleep

Talking to Your Child About Puberty (for Parents). (n.d.). Kids Health.https://kidshealth.org/en/parents/talk-about-puberty.html

Teach your teenager coping skills for wellbeing - ReachOut Parents. (n.d.). https://parents.au.reachout.com/skills-to-build/wellbeing/things-to-try-coping-skills-and-resilience/teach-your-teenager-coping-skills-for-wellbeing

Therapist, L. T. (2018, December 25). Start a teen girl support group.https://losangelesteentherapist.com/how-to-start-a-teen-girls-support-group/

Website, N. (2022, September 13). Early or delayed puberty. nhs.uk.https://www.nhs.uk/conditions/early-or-delayed-puberty/#:~:text=The%20average%20age%20for%20girls,9%20and%2014%20in%20boys.

Printed in France by Amazon
Brétigny-sur-Orge, FR

20844295R00078